Nothing Green

Nothing Green

A Sequel to the Bestselling *Evelyn*

EVELYN DOYLE

ORION

First published in Great Britain in 2003 by
Orion Media
An imprint of the Orion Publishing Group Ltd
Orion House, 5 Upper St Martin's Lane, London WC2H 9EA

A CIP catalogue record for this book is available
from the British Library

ISBN: 0 75285 700 2

Printed in Great Britain by
Clays Ltd, St Ives plc

For Michael with love

'Believe me, every man has his secret sorrows,
which the world knows not;
and oftentimes we call a man cold when he is only sad.'

LONGFELLOW

Acknowledgements

Trevor Dolby, Publishing Director at Orion, for his unfailing support and faith in me. For his wonderful sense of humour and his 'ear' when I needed to let off steam. I am honoured to have him as my friend.

The other fantastic staff at Orion – Pandora, Laura, Juliet and, of course, Gaby Young for her heroic publicity and for getting the first book *Evelyn* 'out there'.

Giles Gordon, my agent at Curtis Brown, for his sage advice and for giving me the confidence I needed to go on.

Kate Cooper, foreign sales at Curtis Brown, good luck and congratulations on your new baby. Thanks Kate for being there for me.

Kim Brownlee, my friend, without your help and support this would have been more difficult to do; a huge thank you.

Shiona Livingston, my best friend and 'test audience'. Everyone should have a 'Shiona' in their life.

My brothers, for jogging my memory and unfailing support. A huge thank you to Elsie, my sister-in-law; for your loving pride in me, I am grateful. To Susanne, Kevin's partner, for rearranging bookshelves up and down the country, you are so welcome in our family.

To Nicola, Christopher, Tracy-Jane and Melonie, my darling nieces and nephew my love and gratitude for your loyalty and support.

To Pierce Brosnan and Beau St Clair at Irish Dreamtime, for immortalising my father's heroic achievement on the silver screen, my grateful thanks.

ONE

Poverty is a word that is not used by poor people. We didn't know we were poor because everyone around us was poor and so a little made us feel rich. An empty floor-polish tin filled with soil for playing hopscotch was a treasured toy. Wooden spinning tops decorated with coloured chalk designs and whipped mercilessly were an endless source of competition. A length of rope looped around the lamp-post made a superb swing and was used as a long skipping rope. As the boys kicked a half-deflated old football further up the street we would chant all our favourite rhymes and they were treated to screams of abuse when the ball caught in our rope. Pebbles laid out on the ground in squares were the palaces and mansions we ruled, dressed in our mammies' old dresses and long-abandoned high-heeled shoes. Any visitors foolish enough to step into our world were treated with a mixture of tyranny, dignity and haughty sufferance. Broken prams became carriages pulled by reluctant younger brothers, whose cries of protest were countered by un-queen-like shouts of 'Shut yer gob or you'll get yer ears boxed.'

Mammies would call out that tea was ready and hand out slices of buttered bread thickly coated with sugar or spread with rich brown savoury pork dripping. Our brothers would hide behind walls and concrete bollards waiting for unsuspecting brewery carts pulled by magnificent dray horses decked out with gleaming brasses, and scut along on the back until the driver noticed them and cracked his whip, stinging

1

fingers and forcing the boys to jump back on to the road. Sometimes injury from following traffic would result and broken bones and torn flesh would be repaired at the hospital. The only sympathy from a distraught mammy would be, 'That'll teach you! You fecking bowsie, what have I told you?' There would be huge relief that no serious damage had been done and later she would tearfully tell her neighbours, 'God spared my babbie.' They would bless themselves, shake their heads and all agree that 'Boys will be boys.'

My friend Chrissie's new baby brother was very sick and her mammy draped Chrissie's Holy Communion veil over his pram, because 'Even if a fly lands on him, the shock would kill him,' Chrissie told me in a loud whisper. On sunny days we would bump him down the steps and wheel him around very carefully.

Poor Mary Lynch got polio. We didn't see her for ages and when she came home she couldn't walk at all, but her mammy let us take her out in her wheelchair sometimes for a little while. The boys pushed her while we pushed Chrissie's brother and when we were out of sight of the street we would race the boys and Mary. We sometimes won because Mary would be frightened by the speed of the boys and scream for them to slow down to a walk.

Topper was the spaniel dog that belonged to everyone, or so we thought – he went home to the Ryans' house at the end of the day. We treated him just like one of us and even shared our sweets with him and let him have a lick of our Vimto ice pops; but he couldn't eat chewing gum and one of the boys had to pull it out of his mouth because we thought he was choking to death. When we had racing games we were annoyed that he always chose to join the boys' team. One day Topper was knocked down by the Kennedys' bread lorry and Noel, my little brother, carried him – even though he was almost as big as Noel – back to our house, where Mam washed and bandaged his leg. Mrs Ryan kept him in for weeks and told us that we weren't fit to mind him. When he got better he came out to play anyway and was part of the gang again.

One morning we woke to find the field in front of our house full of scruffy-looking horses that had been left by the tinkers. Mam told Noel and me to get the old tin bath that hung on a nail outside the kitchen door and fill it with water to give the horses a drink. I didn't like being near animals, apart from the chickens and the pigs in the convent farm. Noel, on the other hand, was always a brave soldier and had no fear. As a little six-year-old he had tried to lead me past a snarling Jack Russell that had managed to get under the gate of Granny's back garden, though all he achieved was the loss of the backside of his trousers. Granny had heard my screams and rushed at the dog with her sweeping brush, sending it howling from where it came.

Now I begged Mam to send Maurice, another of my brothers, instead of me; I told her I was frightened.

'Don't be so bloody soft,' she said. I took one of the handles of the bath. We staggered under the weight, and the water slopped and sloshed over the sides as we crossed the road on to the field. Mam stood at the hall door urging us to go to the middle of the field where most of the horses were grazing on the sparse grass. Some of the horses were watching and started to canter towards us. I dropped my side of the bath and streaked back to the house screaming at the top of my voice. Noel trailed back to the house, dragging the empty bath behind him, telling Mam that this was a man's job and what use were girls to anyone anyway. Mam took the water herself, but I saw through the window that the horses didn't drink it.

As the summer wore on we found a hedge thick with blackberries and Mam made pies and jam. But when we had a picnic of bread and jam and wild mushrooms we found growing under a tree, she poured huge spoonfuls of caster oil down our throats; we were all very sick for a few days.

I would never know a golden summer like that again.

The year before, Dad had won his fight with the government to get my brothers and me out of the industrial schools. He had sent us to them – me to High Park convent in Dublin, my brothers to a convent in Kilkenny – as a temporary measure while he went to find work in England. On his return, he had found that the state would not release us until we were sixteen. After a battle of nearly two years, he had regained custody of us, and he decided to take only the three oldest boys – Noel, Maurice and John – and me home at first until he got on his feet. My younger brothers, Kevin and Dermot, were to remain in Kilkenny for the time being.

He had been given a Corporation house in Finglas West, a new housing development of neat houses north of Dublin. The four of us filled the little house when we arrived shortly before our first Christmas at home.

What a wonderful Christmas that was! Mam, as Jessie told us to call her, put our first ever Christmas tree in the corner of the living room and she showed us how to make paper chains with crêpe paper to hang from the ceiling. She taught me how to make beautiful paper roses to garland the mantelpiece, and the smell of cooking filled the new house. She and Dad had been working hard to get the new house ready for when we came home. My fears about the house and the new mammy slowly began to disappear. At last the great day arrived. We were woken on the morning by Mam shouting up from the bottom of the stairs in her strange English accent, 'Come on, you lot; breakfast is ready.' It was a friendly shout and we all bolted down the stairs pushing each other out of the way to be first in the kitchen. After breakfast we dived into the living room and scrabbled under the tree for our presents. I got a toy grand piano and Dad taught me to play 'Oh Susanna'.

Granddad came to visit and brought his homemade Christmas pudding and the usual oranges and sixpences. Briefly I thought of my real mother and silently asked Our Lady to make sure she was having as good a day as we were.

On St Stephen's Day Dad piled us all into the small car and drove to a little country road at the end of the airport runway. We ate tomato and egg sandwiches and drank lemonade from small bottles while we watched the aeroplanes taking off and landing. They flew only a few feet above the car and we squealed with fright at the noise and fear that one of the planes would hit the car. We were mightily impressed when Dad told us he had gone all the way to England and back in a plane. We asked him if had he seen heaven while he was up there.

The only job Dad and Granddad could get after Christmas was painting the railings around the Johnstown Park for the Corporation; there were hundreds of four-foot-high metal railings stuck on a low concrete wall right around the park and Dad was very bad-tempered because it was cold and the work was tedious. After a couple of weeks he told Granddad that he was going to England to find proper work; and he would get higher wages there. Mam was upset about being left on her own with just the 'kiddies' for company. She had tried to be friendly to the neighbours but only a couple of them would give her the time of day. We all knew it was because she was English and worse, she was a Protestant, or 'pagan' as most of them called her. When any of the kids outside said anything about Mam to my brothers they were treated to a punch on the face. Soon most of the kids in the street just accepted the fact that we had a different mammy; they all knew she wasn't our real mammy because it had been in the papers all through the year before and we enjoyed a certain 'celebrity' status.

Dad left for England at the end of March and the old lump

came back into my chest. I wondered how long he would be gone and if he would ever come back because he didn't seem to be too upset at going away. After he had given me a quick hug he patted my head and said, 'Mind your brothers and help your mammy. Be a good girl.'

He gave Mam a long hug and kissed her on the mouth before getting into his car and driving off. I didn't like it one little bit; I had never seen him kissing or hugging my real mother.

When Dad had gone I missed him and I worried about him being in England all alone. Mam would read some of his letters to us and always there was a little message reminding me that I was the eldest and to 'help your mammy'. Mam told me over and over again that I was 'dirty' and when the boys were allowed out to play she kept me in to show me how to do the 'housework'. I really didn't mind too much. I used to have to do chores in the convent and the nuns had told us that it was to be our privilege in life to look after the home and family, so I felt important. I tried to please her because Dad wanted me to, although I felt miserable and ashamed when she called me 'dirty'.

I went to the school in Dorset Street at the bottom of the road that Granddad lived on. Getting there involved a twenty-minute bus journey that cost a penny each way and I had to take a penny on Mondays for 'the black babies'. Mam didn't think that she should give money to the church when things were so tight at home, so sometimes she didn't give me the penny and I would cry all the way to school on the bus because I knew I would get the strap from the priest who came to collect the money at school. 'You're a miserable uncharitable little wretch,' he would pant with each of the six strokes, his face red with temper, and he promised those of us who hadn't got the penny 'eternal purgatory'. If any of us were foolish enough to admit to not having been to Mass on

Sunday, his rage knew no bounds. When the weather got warmer Mam told me that I would have to do without socks. When a girl who got my bus asked me why I had no socks, I told her, 'My feet get too hot.'

I was desperate for Dad to come home. I seemed to be outside the family. My brothers spent most of their time out in the street playing with their pals, and Mam always had something for me to do in the house.

A few weeks after he had left, Mam read Dad's letter and told us, 'Your father's money hasn't arrived', and that we would have to 'make do' with what food we had left from the last week. We knew that she hadn't had her cigarettes for a couple of days and we noticed that she didn't eat with us at mealtimes. We didn't get a letter from Dad for a couple of weeks after that, and Mam was becoming more and more bad-tempered. She would stand at the door watching the postman come along the street and when he passed by he would call out to her, 'Nothing today missus, sorry,' and wish her 'the top o' the morn'. Mam's mouth would form a thin hard line and she would slam things about for a little while.

At last a letter with an English stamp plopped through the letterbox. Dad had written that he was sorry but it had taken him longer to get work than he had hoped and all he could spare was a couple of pounds. Mam rubbed her forehead and I thought she was going to cry, but she took a deep breath, straightened her shoulders and said, 'Right kids, we have to have a council of war.'

She made being hungry and broke sound like some sort of game we would all have to play. We were to go on to the many building sites all around and collect wood for the fire, and she was going to go into the city centre and get as much as she could with the money Dad had sent. At first it was fun filling old potato sacks with wood and being chased by workmen. I hoped that I wouldn't have to find another Mr Gleason. He

EVELYN DOYLE

was the terrible dirty old man who paid me threepence for tea and currant chests we begged from Mr Hennessey who owned the little shop in Fatima Mansions where we lived before my real mother left us. Mam made a dish called 'scouse' with potatoes, onions and a minute amount of neck of lamb, which we liked it. Sometimes she got a big parcel of what she called 'liver and lites' from the butcher for about a shilling. She also made barley pudding, which was like rice pudding but made with pearl barley, and she would try to make it taste better by putting custard powder in it; it was awful but we ate it because we were hungry and we tried not to make funny faces about it if she was looking. In the evenings we all sat on the floor round the wireless that Dad had made himself, and listened to *Life with the Lyons*, an American comedy programme, and we heard a very English voice telling us, 'This is the BBC Home Service' and what the next programme would be. We couldn't understand how his voice came all the way over the sea from England and we asked if Dad could talk on the wireless.

One day I was very hungry and I took a slice of bread and spread it with margarine and a spoonful of sugar and sat on the back door step to eat it. Mam came up behind me and snatched it from my hand. 'You're a little thief!' She was really angry. She told me to go to bed for a punishment. 'There'll be no tea or breakfast for you, lady!' She pushed me up the stairs. I was confused and ashamed at the same time; she hadn't told me that I couldn't have a piece of bread, and how could I steal bread from my own house? It was a sin to steal and now I would have to confess to the priest on Saturday that I had stolen bread. God! How many Hail Marys would this cost me? Mam didn't shout or hit us; it was always bed 'and no tea or supper' for up to three days depending on the 'crime', and there was rarely remission.

Mam heard that there was money to be made picking potatoes in the country and that the farmers even sent a lorry to take workers to the fields. We all helped to make a picnic of jam sandwiches and lemonade and set off at four in the morning. We waited for what seemed like hours at the end of the road but no lorry turned up; we were waiting at the wrong end of the road. We returned home, cold, tired and miserable. Mam said nothing but her lips formed a thin hard line.

Shortly after that Dad came home. Mam had written to him and told him that she was going home to England and he had better come back and look after his 'kiddies'. She wasn't prepared to stay in a country where she couldn't feed the children in her care and where she couldn't even get a job or find the 'right end of a bloody road' when the possibility of work turned up. Dad stayed home and got work painting more railings, which made him very bad-tempered. Sometimes he got work painting the new houses at the sites where we had collected wood, and he would be his old happy self again.

One night Dad sent me for his evening paper. When I got to the shop I got a terrible shock: there on the counter was a row of newspapers with my photograph on the front page of them all, and a follow-up story from the year before. The press people had obviously photographed me while I was out playing. I bolted back across the field and burst into the house slamming the door behind me. I stood with my back to the door breathless and crying; my legs were like jelly. When I was able to tell Dad what I'd seen he roared like an angry bear, 'The fecking bastards! Are they never going to leave us alone?'

A few weeks later Dad went back to England and Mam told us that we were going to join him when he got a house. I told Mam that I was not going to England, a land of pagans, and in any case I couldn't leave Ireland without my baby brothers, Kevin and Dermot, who were still in the convent in Kilkenny.

'Your father will come back for them as soon as we are settled,' she told me. She always referred to Dad as 'your father'.

When he was in a bad mood she would say, 'Your father's seen his arse.' Dad would be most offended by this remark and not speak to her for a few hours. Mam had some weird and wonderful phrases that even when she was angry with us would make us laugh out loud. When any of the boys were cheeky to her she would yell out, 'I'll clat your bluddy ear 'ole, ye cheeky bugger!' She never did 'clat' anyone's 'ear 'ole'.

For the next few months while Dad was in England she struggled to feed and clothe us. We would walk with her all the way into Dublin city centre and rake around the flea markets for clothes and wait at the end of the day at the food stalls and pick up cheap vegetables and fruit.

Sometimes she had a couple of shillings to spare and would buy a slab of snow cake for a treat and a neck of lamb to make a big pot of stew. I don't think Dad was ever aware of just how poor he kept us. Did he really believe that £3 or £4 a week would feed and clothe us all? Mam certainly never bought new clothes for herself, and she had to recycle her cigarettes, carefully taking the thin paper off the butts and saving the tobacco in a jam-jar to make roll-ups.

As the summer passed we children were rarely in the house; even I was allowed out when the days got longer. Granddad would visit two or three times a week and bring his home-made bread; and although he still called Mam 'Mrs Brown' he would bring her a packet of Sweet Afton cigarettes and give her a half crown for a bag of coal, and he always had a barley sugar twist for us all. Mam didn't buy coal with the money Granddad gave her; she used the money for food and we still went on the building sites for wood.

One day when we went to a site a workman was eating his lunch in the sunshine. We stood gazing at him as he munched on huge sandwiches with slices of thick ham hanging over the sides of the bread. Suddenly he wrapped his lunch back into the paper and put it into my hand. 'Here!

Have them,' he said. He sounded exactly like Mr Hennessey when he gave us the tea and currant chests. 'Now feck off before you get hurt. This is no place for bairns.'

We raced home with the precious parcel and even Mam joined in the feast.

Towards the end of summer Dad sent for us; we were to get the mail boat to Liverpool from Dublin quays the following Thursday night. My brothers were very excited to be going on a boat all the way to England. I wasn't too sure. I had made friends and was settled, and besides my baby brothers were only two hours away down in the country. Not only was England a faraway land full of strange people who were all Protestant pagans, but my real mother would never be able to find us if she ever wanted to come back.

Mary Rooney, who lived next door, told me that the English didn't ring out the Angelus so you had to try to remember what time it was by yourself. Dan, her brother who worked in London, had told her, 'There's black men who kidnap Irish Catholic girls for the white slave trade.' I said I would be careful; I didn't want to work in a laundry for the rest of my life. I knew it would be the laundries because I had heard a woman in the convent laundry say she was 'just a fecking slave here'. 'How will I know one?' I asked her. I couldn't imagine what a black man looked like. Though we had been taking a penny to school every Monday morning for as long as I could remember, as had every school child in Ireland, for the 'black babies' in Africa, it had never occurred to us that they grew up to be people. 'Oh, you'll know them right away – they have huge potato sacks over their shoulders.'

When I asked Mam about the black slavers she told me not to be 'bloody stupid' and carried on with the business of packing for our great journey. The boys had been dispatched to the shops to find large cardboard boxes into which went everything we owned except our shoes and Wellington boots; these went into a large expanding string bag. Mam tied each box with thick twine and made loops for handles. We had dismantled Dad's homemade wireless and hidden all the parts and valves among the blankets and sheets in case the English customs took it. Mam said there wasn't enough room for what few toys we had; in fact the only thing we wanted to take was a one-legged teddy bear we had found a few weeks earlier. We had taken him to the Garda in the old village and the nice garda there told us that we could keep him if no one claimed him. Every day for six weeks we all walked to the village to check if the teddy had been claimed until finally we were able to take him home. The garda said 'Thank God!' as we ran from the station, fearful that he would change his mind and take the teddy back. He couldn't come with us; I gave him to Mary Rooney.

On Thursday morning a man came and took our furniture away on a horse and cart. He gave Mam £10 for the whole lot and agreed to take our boxes to the mail boat. When it was getting dark we closed the blue front door and left like thieves in the night. No one from our street came to say goodbye to us. Granddad met us at the boat. Our boxes were on the cobbled quayside at his feet. It was very cold and icy rain was stinging our legs. Granddad asked a young man to help Mam take the boxes on to the boat and gave him half a crown for his trouble. He patted the boys' heads and told them to remember that they would always be Irishmen no matter how long they were away from 'our green land'; and as he hugged me he said, 'Goodnight, my dear child. "Parting is such sweet sorrow / That I should say goodnight till it be morrow".' Granddad always had a saying or quotation for every occasion. He pressed a little St Christopher medal into my hand to 'keep you safe' until he could get over to 'the accursed place', as he called England. I was going to miss him so much. He shook hands with Mam and we walked up the wooden ramp on to the mail boat.

It seemed as though the whole of Dublin was there, waving and shouting goodbye and reminding loved ones to write soon. Old women held younger women as they cried together and children sheltered under their mammies' coats to keep warm. As the boat steamed out of the bay, Granddad stood at another part of the quays, all alone, waving his big white hankie. A big lump filled my throat as I waved back shouting, 'Bye, Granddad' at the top of my voice. He looked so lonely and I wished he was coming with us. I wondered if Our Lady would come all the way to England with me; I hoped she would.

Mam and the boys had found a long bench in the covered passenger deck and carefully pushed the boxes up against the seat so that no one would trip over them. After we had eaten the jam sandwiches Mam had made before we left Finglas we huddled together. A kind crewman brought some coats and laid them over us. Soon most of the passengers were sleeping on the other seats that were scattered all over the deck. A group of five or six men were playing a game of cards through a cloud of cigarette smoke in a far corner. We were too excited to sleep and too afraid that someone would pinch our boxes – after all, they were all we owned in the world. Mam dozed on and off throughout the night.

Finally the boat stopped. Some men helped us with our boxes as we followed the stream of people off the boat into an enormous shed with a glass roof; Mam kept reminding us, 'Keep together, you lot.' The noise was deafening. There was black soot and thick dirt clinging to the roof and the tiled walls. Thousands of people hurried to and fro, some going towards the boat and some going our way; young men were running too and hugging and twirling young women who were crying with joy at being reunited with loved ones. Most of them appeared to be shouting at the tops of their voices, which echoed right up to the glass roof. A group of girls wearing bright red berets and royal blue blazers and led by a very pretty lady were weaving through the crowds; they were like little dancing poppies making their way through the huge sea of drab greys and browns. We couldn't understand the strange accents we heard. A train was huffing and hissing somewhere near by, and through it all I could hear a man whistling 'Kathleen Mavurneen'. I thought of Ireland and how I missed it already. The men dropped our boxes on the concrete floor and when Mam offered them a coin they refused politely and raised their caps to her. One of them said, 'You'll be needing it more than us, Mother.'

Mam told us to stay where we were and not to move, and went off to find Dad. My brothers and I surrounded the boxes and formed a little island amid the chaos. After a while Mam came back and told us that Dad hadn't been able to come for us but we were not to worry as he would be in Manchester when we got there. She had managed to get hold of a two-wheeled porter's barrow and after a struggle we piled the boxes on top of each other on it, Maurice was detailed to carry the string bag bulging with the shoes.

We joined a queue in the customs shed and watched with growing alarm as uniformed officers opened the cases and boxes of the people in front of us. They would surely find Dad's wireless, even if it was in bits. We all held a bit of Mam's coat skirt as our turn came.

'You'll 'ave to give me an 'and; the kiddies can't manage,' Mam said to the officer. Her English accent became stronger and she dropped all her aitches.

He came from the other side of the long table and marked our boxes with a big blue chalk cross. As he waved us through, he told Mam, 'I shouldn't think there's much to interest me in that lot, love.'

Maurice, feeling very important, offered up the string bag to the officer for inspection and the kind man smiled as he put a large blue cross on the sole of one of the shoes that was sticking out at the bottom.

'There y'are, cocker, not much chance of 'iding contraband in there, eh?' He seemed to talk through his nose and he cut his words very short. We thought it was very funny that he called Mam 'love' and Maurice didn't look anything like a spaniel.

Mam pushed the barrow while the boys helped to balance the boxes as we made our way out of the shed towards the train, which was hissing and steaming, waiting to take us to our new life.

TWO

The row of red-brick terraced houses on either side of the narrow street seemed to stretch into infinity. There were no gardens or even a tree in sight; in fact there was nothing green on Oxford Street, where Dad had bought a tiny house. Smoke belched out of the squat brick chimneys and a yellow fog swirled around the grey-slated rooftops.

Dad had collected us from the train station in Mam's brother's car. We were squashed in the back with two of the boxes and Mam sat in the front passenger seat. Now we were standing on the pavement outside one of the houses about halfway down the street. Dad was telling Mam, 'I know it's not much to look at, but we'll do it up.' Mam just wanted to get us all in off the cold grey street and fill her blue-and-white-striped pint mug with hot tea.

Dad was right. The house wasn't much to look at inside either. The rooms were small, cold and fusty. The kitchen door opened on to a tiny concrete yard and we were separated from the neighbours on either side by a high brick wall. I had expected there to be a little garden, but the only plants were sparse weeds trying to push through the cracks on one of the walls. At the bottom of the yard there was an old dilapidated wooden hut.

'I'm not going in that!' I declared to Dad when I saw that the 'hut' was in fact an outside lavie. I didn't know that there was a small bathroom upstairs in the house.

Mam told me that I would do as I was 'bloody told' and like

it. 'Beggars can't be choosers, so get off your high 'orse, madam.'

I was stung by the bitterness in her voice and surprised that Dad took her side.

'You just listen to your mammy and do what she tells you, did you hear me?'

A feeling of dread came over me; Dad hadn't even hugged me when he met us at the train station and he seemed not to be bothered by Mam's harshness towards me. Ireland and home seemed so far away now.

We were all enrolled at local schools within a couple of weeks of arriving; the boys went to the primary school and I was sent to an all-girls secondary modern about a mile away. It was a Protestant school and I worried constantly about my soul. When I muttered my prayers some of the girls in my class sniggered, but most of them were really kind and they all admired my beautiful rosary beads that the Reverend Mother at the convent had given me; that was only last year, but it seemed a lifetime ago. My roll number was thirty-three and the class would fall silent as my turn approached to say my number. 'Tirty-tree,' I would mumble and the girls would giggle until the teacher told them to stop and behave. Everything was strange to me. The fact that I had to speak to the teachers in English made my early days hard. I kept forgetting and asking or answering the teacher in Gaelic. The English spoken by my new friends was very foreign to me indeed; none of them pronounced their aitches and words ending with 't' were cut short with a sort of 'hik' sound. I spent hours practising the 'th' sound.

In order to kit us all out for our new schools Mam had spent several Saturday mornings at jumble sales. She had managed to find an outfit that looked vaguely like the school uniform that the other girls at my school wore: an old-fashioned navy-blue gym slip and white shirt, under which went large navy blue knickers for PE and black lace-up shoes that almost fitted – she told me, 'You'll grow into them.' And, most embarrassing of all, she made me wear a dreadful grey full-skirted, much too long coat and grey bowler style hat with a maroon and gold band, obviously the donation by the mother of some rich kid who went to a private school. It was no use appealing to Dad; he seemed to have relinquished responsibility for our care and welfare to Mam. He didn't even comb my hair or put ribbons in it like he used to before our real mother left us. He had become a remote and harsh daddy and hardly spoke to us except to shout at us for disobeying 'orders', as Mam called the rules which we had to live by now. I thought he didn't love me any more, because I seemed to always be 'in trouble'.

One day, not long after we arrived in Manchester, Dad took me into the city centre. I was overjoyed: here we were going out together again on our own. As we started walking along Deansgate I took his hand.

'You're too old for that nonsense now,' he said in a cold voice and brushed my hand away. I started to cry and he told me to 'stop snivelling' and grow up. 'I've brought you here for one thing only,' he said.

As he strode along I had to trot to keep up with him, but he didn't slow down. At last he stopped and pointed across the road. 'Do you see him?' He was pointing at a large black man who was cleaning the windows of a pub on the other side of the road. The man had a big kind face and smiled at people passing by, showing a row of sparkling perfect white teeth, and his head was covered by tight woolly looking black hair. He was the first black man I had ever seen and I thought he was magnificent.

'Don't ever feel sorry for one of them, do you hear me?' Dad was very serious. 'They can look pathetic and it's easy to feel sorry for them.' The expression on his face prevented me from asking him why. Was he one of the slavers Mary Rooney had told me about, I wondered, even though he didn't have a potato sack anywhere near him?

Mam and Dad started to argue a lot and we could hear that it was nearly always about money. On one occasion Mam said she was going to find a job.

'You've got a bloody job, looking after me and my kids,' Dad was shouting at the top of his voice.

Mam sat on the edge of her chair, hunched forward with her hands hanging limply between her parted knees; her face had no expression. After a long pause she pointed at me and said in her flat slow monotone voice, 'That one is old enough to pull 'er weight.' She reached up to the mantelpiece for the large jam-jar filled with the tobacco saved from her and Dad's butts and rolled a thin cigarette. As far as she was concerned that was the end of the matter.

The lump came back into my chest. Memories of Fatima Mansions flooded into my mind. I feared having to be responsible for everyone as I was then and I couldn't imagine going back to that. The two years in the convent had taught me to be a child. But although Mam didn't like me, she looked after us all.

I became 'that one' to Dad and Mam; I tried to be good and do everything I was told, and I kept out of the way as much as possible, but it was no use – Mam didn't like me and Dad rarely spoke to me. On the odd occasion when he showed any sign of affection or kindness to me Mam would start a row. It was all a complete mystery and I was confused and miserable. I longed to be back in the convent, where even harsh words were softly spoken and where I didn't have to try hard to be liked.

Mam's mother came to stay. She was a very old woman and she disliked me even more than Mam did. I had to share my bed with her. I clung to the edge of the bed trying not to touch her in any way and when I was sure she was asleep I would lie on a coat on the floor. The nightmares I'd suffered in the convent came back.

One day I walked into the kitchen and realised that Mam and her mother were rowing about something. I heard Mam say something about the 'kiddie'. They immediately stopped talking when they saw me. Mam told me, 'Get out of 'ere and mind your own bloody business!' To her mother she said, 'That one's a sly little bugger.' I fled to my room and cried. I decided that I must get away but I was only twelve years old and had nowhere to go. I formed a plan in my mind. Mam was always threatening to have me sent back to the convent and I thought that if I did something really bad Dad would let her do it.

As I dressed for school the following morning I saw the old woman's purse on the chair in my bedroom. The old woman was snoring her head off, her toothless mouth wide open; the sight of her made me shudder. I opened the purse and took out a ten-shilling note. Sweat was running down my back and my hands were shaking as I rolled the note into a long cigar shape and tucked it tightly into the band of my grey hat. I hadn't a clue what I would do with ten shillings if Mam didn't find out that I had it; it was a fortune. I hid in the lavie at the bottom of the yard until it was time for school. As I got to the front door I heard Mam calling, 'Come back here you!' My brothers had already left for school and I knew it was me she was talking to. I felt sick, and I was shaking inside as I entered the living room. Mam and her mother were sitting on either side of the fireplace; the old woman was on the rocking chair, gently rocking back and forth with one slippered foot tapping rhythmically on the green and orange flower-patterned lino. They looked like a pair of hungry crows.

Mam told me to empty my school satchel on the floor. 'You're a little thief, aren't you?'

The quiet and calm of her voice frightened me; by now I was shaking from head to foot and couldn't hide it. She made me take off all my clothes while she searched them. I crossed my arms in front of my skinny naked body, ashamed and humiliated but worried that she wouldn't find the ten-shilling note; I couldn't tell her where to look.

She said to her mother, 'Are you sure you 'ad it?' Her mother assured her that she had drawn her pension the day before and she was positive that there were two ten-shilling notes in her purse before she went to bed.

Mam told me to get dressed and she raked in my school satchel again. She told me to get out. Just as I was leaving she called me back and snatched the hat off my head. As Mam pulled at the hat band, I silently asked Our Lady to forgive me for stealing and for going to a Protestant school and to stay with me when I was sent back to the convent.

'Yes! I took her old money, so just send me back to the convent,' I shouted at Mam. I had nothing to lose now and couldn't help myself. 'I hate you! I hate you! You're not my real mother.' I fled from the room to the lavie and bolted the door.

I didn't go to school that day. Mam told me to go to my room and wait for 'your father'. I stayed there all day; she gave me nothing to eat. When Dad came home she didn't tell him; I did.

'So now you can send me back to the nuns,' I sobbed.

Dad's face softened; he knelt down on one knee in front of me and held my hands, the first time for a long while that he had actually touched me.

'Ebbs, you just don't understand how things are. We need her, and you have got to stop fighting her.' He wouldn't believe me when I told him that I was trying really hard to get her to like me. 'She'll never like you, and when you grow up I'll tell you why; you wouldn't understand now.' He went on to explain that in a few weeks' time he was going to Ireland to get Kevin and Dermot out of the convent in Kilkenny before 'the bastard brothers' – Dad's expression for the notorious Christian Brothers schools in Ireland, where boys from the convent went when they turned eleven – got them, and he couldn't do it if Mam wasn't with us. He patted my head before he left the room and I felt that my Daddy loved me again.

School became a happy place as I settled in and got used to the strange English girls. Three of my friends were called Carol, one of whom used to buy me a 'wagon wheel' chocolate biscuit from the tuck shop at mid-morning playtime. Another friend, Kay, brought me thick buttered toast wrapped in greaseproof paper almost every morning. All my friends had money to spend at the tuck shop, but although Dad was scrupulous about giving us our threepenny-bit pocket money on Saturday mornings, we had no money to spend through the week. Sometimes we would find an empty pop bottle and get the threepence deposit back from a shop, but that was a rare find. Slowly I realised that compared to my friends at school we were poor. None of them had more than one or two brothers and sisters; none of them could imagine having five brothers and when I told them that our family was a small one by Irish standards, they shook their heads and declared that they would have only one baby when they grew up and got married.

The walk home from school was a pleasant meander through some of the better streets in our district. I would keep an eye on the progress of the spring flowers as they pushed their spiky shoots through the hard frosty soil in the neat gardens, and watch the leaf buds fatten on the bare brown branches of the flowering cherry and lilac trees. In summer I would breathe deeply the glorious scent of roses and lavender. As the chill of frost invaded in the autumn, I would shuffle through the crunchy brown leaves that carpeted the pavements and know that another year was nearly over, which meant that I was that much nearer to being a grown-up, when I would escape the oppressive atmosphere at home.

The pretty streets all too soon gave way to the barren narrow streets where we lived. And each time I turned the corner into Oxford Street, my heart would give a little jump when I saw Dad's Ford Anglia parked in the distance outside our door. Fear would grip my heart and my mouth would become dry as I tried to remember if I had forgotten to do something that was part of my before-school chores. I hated going up the street and my feet became leaden as I trudged, as slow as I dared, to the house.

One dark, cold day as I approached the house with the usual dread I could hear a cello. The sad strains of 'Vilia' from *The Merry Widow* operetta floated towards me.

'Granddad, Granddad!' I shouted as I raced along the uneven flag-stoned pavement to the house, all fear magically lifted from my mind. He heard me and was at the front door when I reached it.

'Let me look at you! My, how you've grown.' Granddad knelt down on one knee and hugged me to him as I threw myself at him. The dear familiar smell of mothballs, tobacco, liquorice and Pears soap that was Granddad permeated my senses and comforted me; I immediately burst into tears. I hadn't had a loving hug since he had hugged me goodbye at Dublin quays all those months ago. I hadn't had many hugs in the convent but that didn't matter as none of us got hugs and I hadn't felt as unwanted or unloved as I had for so much of the time since we had come to live in England. My Granddad had come to live with us and now that he was here he would look out for me and everything would be right again.

Mam's mother and Granddad didn't like each other at all.

Granddad referred to her as 'that dirty oul' one' and Mam's mother called Granddad "is lordship'. One day they had a shouting match. The old woman had washed all the socks in the house; there were dozens of them and she had hung them all over the place to dry: along the mantelpiece where an unpleasant-smelling steam went up the wall and snaked along the ceiling leaving white trails in the nicotine stains, over the chairs and even draped from the windowsills, causing little puddles to form on the floor. This was too much for Granddad and he went behind her snatching up the socks and throwing them in a ball into a corner of the room. He then sat serenely reading his paper. He winked at me from behind the pages as the old woman stormed into the kitchen. I giggled out loud.

Mam came into the room, pointed at me and, using the harsh voice she usually used when addressing me, ordered, 'You! Pick them bloody socks up.'

I jumped to do as I was bidden but Granddad stopped me. He asked Mam who the hell she was talking to. 'You will not use that tone to my granddaughter, and kindly use her name,' he said in his best autocratic tone. My appearance had not gone unnoticed by him. My hair was greasy and lank, my skin grey and drawn, and my clothes smelly and obviously old; the only underwear I had was the vest and the navy blue knickers she had bought me when I started school.

Mam's mother immediately jumped to her daughter's defence and told Granddad not to speak to her daughter like that.

I ran to the lavie in the yard and hid until the row was over, begging Our Lady not to let Granddad go away.

When Dad came home, there was another row about having 'that dirty oul' biddy' in his house. Mam's mother left the next day.

How strange my little brothers were when they came home.

They had funny country accents and marched everywhere, swinging their arms smartly. Dad had to keep telling them to walk quietly. They had never seen a girl before, only women and nuns, and hid behind Dad when he told them to say hello to me; they didn't know that they had a sister. Dad had made a big cake and decorated it with white icing and 'Welcome home boys' written in blue on the top. My real mother had taught him how to bake and decorate cakes; she had been a master confectioner before she married Dad.

The little house was filled to overflowing now, and Mam and Dad became more and more bad-tempered. Mam had got a job in the canteen of a jam factory in Trafford Park and had to leave the house before six in the morning; she didn't get home until well after six in the evening. When Dad was in a particularly bad temper we would stand at the bus stop and wait for Mam to come home, and let her go into the house first, knowing that she would calm Dad down before we followed her inside a few minutes later. Sometimes Mam didn't come home from work at all, but would be in bed a couple of mornings later when I took Dad his morning tea. We had no idea where she had been or why she went missing for a few days periodically but we didn't dare ask. Dad would be in a foul temper until she was back. For a little while after her return she would be a bit nicer to me, but within a couple of weeks she would turn on me again. I often wished she wouldn't bother coming home at all.

Dad worked on and off but it seemed that he was at home more than at work. He found it difficult to get on with most people whom he worked with, especially when they nicknamed him 'Paddy' as they invariably did. He was very unhappy living in England. One day he tried to get sacked from a job by sitting smoking under a 'no smoking' sign; he failed because he was one of the best painters his employers had ever had. When he was not working he spent his days playing the piano; after Granddad came to live with us, he played his cello with Dad. When Dad didn't have a job he would earn money in the evenings in a pub playing the piano for £5 a week and as much beer as he could drink. Usually he would be in a filthy temper the following morning, complaining that he must have had 'a bad bottle'.

My brothers and I had to do most of the housework and make breakfast. Dad considered housework beneath him: it was women's work. It had to be done before we went to school, we three oldest taking turns in the 'back kitchen' as Mam called it. She rationed the food very carefully. She marked on the milk bottle how much milk we could use, but we just used more and filled the bottle back to the level of the mark with water; there were always twenty-four slices of bread to a loaf – we couldn't cheat on that one but we took turns having the heel end because it was thicker; and we were introduced to the 'flat spoon' of sugar and tea. We were soon as lean but not as fit as butchers' dogs. Dad, being the 'man' of the house, had to have the best meat and vegetables. That was the Irish way in those days. He insisted that all his vegetables were peeled and Mam saved the carrot peelings to put in a stew for us. We didn't mind too much; most of our nourishment came from free school dinners and the gill of milk we got at school.

Dad rented a television, the first we had ever seen. The day it was delivered we sat mesmerised watching *Andy Pandy* and something called a 'cricket test match'; what a wonderful place this England was when we could have the pictures in our house. Our viewing was strictly rationed to children's half-hour between five and five thirty; we were then banished to the back kitchen until bedtime at half past seven, just in case 'something unsuitable' should sully our young minds. 'Something unsuitable' to Dad meant any suggestion that a man and woman might kiss, and if it looked as though they were going to kiss, he would jump off his chair and run to the television to switch it off and shout about 'the dirty bastards'. But when he was out at the pub Mam sometimes let us older ones watch some programmes such as *Dixon of Dock Green* and *Rawhide*; my brothers whistled the theme tune to *Dixon of Dock Green* to warn each other if Dad was about to catch them at anything they shouldn't be doing. We were not allowed to play out in the street. Dad thought the English streets were not safe for children and in any case there weren't many children our age living near us – not that any English children would have anything much to do with a gang of scruffy Irish kids. Apart from school and running to the shops for Dad and Mam, the only time we got out was on Sunday afternoons, when no matter what the weather was, my brothers and I had to get out of the house for the afternoon and go for a walk. We usually went to the local park, where there were swings, roundabouts and slides and in the summer we would listen to the bands that played there in the pretty round red bandstand. On really wet and cold days we sat in the shelters, where old men passed the time of day. Sometimes we were the only people in the park apart from the 'parky', who would chase us out at four o'clock. ''Avn't you lot an 'ome t' go t'?' he would say, and we would have to walk around the streets until it was time to go back to the house.

One day we were looking in a sweet shop window, sheltering from the cold drizzle under the green-and-white-striped canvas canopy, choosing what we would have if we were rich and could spend a whole pound on whatever we wanted. We got very excited choosing what we thought would be the most expensive sweets in the tall sparkling jars lined up in the window. I was going to buy a half pound of coconut mushrooms and some Pontefract cakes for Granddad; the boys wanted the yellow and black bullseyes, sherbet lemons, pyramid-shaped frozen orange jubilees and of course that most unattainable of all, the king of sweets, a Mars bar. We stopped shouting when we saw a very posh lady going into the shop and watched through the window as she bought a huge box of chocolates. When she came out of the shop she paused and looked at us then turned to go on her way, but she changed her mind and came back to where we were standing, still watching her. By the look on her face I thought we had done something wrong, but she smiled sadly at us and handed me a two-shilling piece. 'Buy some toffees, love,' she said and walked quickly away. I told my brothers that we must remember to say a special Hail Mary for this lady; she was so nice, she must have been a Catholic.

The back kitchen was where my brothers and I formed our very close bond, talking in low whispers, planning our lives for the future and trawling over the past and our lives as they used to be in the convents. Kevin and Dermot were confused and bewildered by this thing called family life, in which we were constantly shouted at and often felt Dad's hand across our ears, and in which at the weekends we were hungry because there were no school dinners. We didn't seem to be able to do anything right and found ourselves in bed with no tea or supper on a regular basis. Sometimes a piece of bread and jam could be smuggled upstairs to the unfortunate victim of a real or imagined misdemeanour; if Granddad was about he would intervene and tell Mam and Dad that they were cruel. A huge row would follow and the atmosphere in the house would be awful for days afterwards.

Mam seemed to hate Dermot almost as much as she did me, but the rest of us tried to look out for him. Dad had forbidden us to do school homework and told the schools that if they couldn't teach us what we needed to know through the day that was too bad, that we had other obligations at home; yet he demanded of us that we all stay in the A stream. Thank God we were all about two years ahead of the rest of our class because of our convent education. One day Noel didn't come home from school at the usual time. As the minutes ticked away Dad got angrier and angrier, shouting what he would do to that 'bowsie' when he got home. At about five o'clock it was dark and still there was no sign of Noel. Dad slammed out of the house and drove like a madman to the school, where he was informed that Noel was in detention for letting off a fire extinguisher. Dad found the classroom and burst in. The teacher, who was only about five foot two inches tall, didn't stand a chance. Dad grabbed him by the throat and demanded to know why he was keeping a child back when it was dark. 'He has a fecking busy road to cross, you bastard,' he roared at the unfortunate man and dropped him back into his chair. The Doyle boys were never again given detention. Dad wasn't really worried about Noel crossing the road; it was more to do with Noel being behind with his household chores and the possibility of Dad having to empty the ashes from the fire grate and bring coal up from the cellar himself.

Granddad stayed mainly in his room when we came home from school, but we could 'visit' him for a few minutes, when he would remind us that we were 'proud Irishmen' and must never forget it in this 'godforsaken land'. He insisted that we spoke to him in Gaelic. He would wander downstairs with an old sweaty sock wrapped around his head: Granddad's cure for headaches. If there was any noise he would tell the boys that they were 'young bowsies who had no consideration for their elders'. Granddad never choked me off, and he protected me as much as he could from Mam's sharp tongue.

My happiest times were with Granddad when he started to teach me to play the piano. We would have 'the parlour' to ourselves for a couple of hours twice a week. Mam complained that I was getting behind with my housework; Granddad told her that my musical education was more important than dusting and washing snotty handkerchiefs. She might think that

George Bernard Shaw was correct when he said, 'Home is the girl's prison and the woman's workhouse.' 'Well, not for my granddaughter it won't be!' he declared and waved his hand, dismissing her from the parlour.

Dad was teaching Noel and Maurice to play the clarinet; Noel wasn't too keen and stubbornly refused to 'flatten' his cheeks or practise. Dad would roar at him, 'Do you want to play this bloody thing or not?' One night Noel said that he didn't want to play anything. Dad shouted at him that he was 'a fecking waster' and boxed his ears. Noel thought it was worth it, as afterwards Dad stopped teaching him and he no longer had to practise scales and exercises for hours on end, and we all admired him for his courage in standing up to Dad. Maurice, on the other hand, was a gifted and dedicated musician and could be heard halfway down the street practising for hours in front of the open bedroom window. Later on he won a place at the grammar school and a scholarship to the prestigious Northern School of Music in Manchester. However, when he was offered a place in the Huddersfield Symphony Orchestra (which was run by a very well-known composer) when he was only fifteen, Dad refused to let him take the place saying that he was 'too young'. The three younger boys were ignored as far as their musical education was concerned.

I was nearly thirteen and our third Christmas in this cold, grey city was fast approaching. Mam looked tired and ill when we brought up the subject of putting up Christmas decorations. She said that there would be no decorations this year. 'We've too many bloody bills to pay. I know your father is working, but God knows 'ow long that will last!' she explained to us. We didn't argue – that was not allowed – but we knew that we might get some presents if Dad could just hold on to his job for a few more weeks. School was a gay, happy place at this time of the year and I had been given a small part in the Christmas play. I was to play the crippled boy's mother in *The Pied Piper*. Then there was the school Christmas party to look forward to.

One day about three weeks before Christmas my mind was full of happy thoughts as I walked home from school. Reaching our house I heard the most fearful row going on just behind the hall door. Dad and Granddad had rowed before, but this was different. They were saying terrible things to each other and Granddad was cursing. I clamped my hand over my mouth and tried to hear what it was all about.

'Oh please, Holy Mother, don't let Granddad leave us,' I begged silently as I fingered the rosary beads that I kept around my neck hidden by my school shirt. Dad called Granddad 'a fecking interfering old bastard' and roared, 'Get out! Go on, get out, I don't ever want to see you again!' I was beside myself with panic; surely it would blow over – it was nearly Christmas after all. Granddad said something in Gaelic but I couldn't make it out, then, 'Evelyn's not responsible for any of it. Nobody forced that bloody woman to go with you, but you stand idly by, allowing her to treat my granddaughter like a skivvy. Don't you think she's been through enough already?'

What had I done? Cold sweat ran down the small of my back and I started to shake like a leaf. What did Dad think I was responsible for? I leaned against the door frame, too afraid to go into the house. Suddenly the door was yanked open and I nearly fell into the hall. Granddad came out on to the street, carrying his brown leather Gladstone bag. Dad was right behind him. Both their faces were white; they were breathing heavily and their eyes looked wild.

Dad saw me and pulled me into the house by the collar of my coat with, 'Get in here, you.'

Granddad told him to take his hands off me and put his

bag on the path. He came into the hall, pulled me from Dad and held me close.

'I have to go back to Ireland, my pet. This accursed English damp is no good for my old bones; goodbye and God bless.' He walked out of the front door, telling me to mind his cello and draw the bow across the strings occasionally, and then he was gone.

I cried, 'Don't go, Granddad. Please don't go.' I wanted to follow him. I watched his retreating ramrod-straight back from the doorway as he walked smartly down the wet, windswept street and my world fell apart; my teacher, my protector was gone.

Dad told me to go to my room. As I hung my coat up in the hall press, Mam passed me. She had been crying. I wanted to ask her what was wrong but she gave me a malevolent look that told me that she hated me.

My nightmares came back to haunt me that night. I was sitting in the middle of a very wide shallow concrete stairway holding a tightly wrapped bundle; as I unfolded the layers off the bundle the flesh on the body of a tiny baby fell away like cooked chicken off the skeleton. I woke up sweating and crying and for a second or two wondered if my baby brother Dermot had survived being burned in his pram during that dreadful year before my real mother had left us.

I didn't hear from or see Granddad ever again.

THREE

In the days that followed Granddad's departure there was an air of desolation in the already gloomy house and we crept about doing our housework and speaking in whispers, while Mam sat in the living room smoking and drinking cold tea from her blue-and-white-striped pint mug; she sat like a man, leaning forward, her elbows on her knees, which hung apart, mug in one hand and cigarette in the other.

One night I lay in bed, waiting for Dad to come back from the pub. I had made his supper as usual and left it covered in the cold cupboard. It never varied: two shelled hard-boiled eggs, a sliced tomato, three cold pork sausages and three slices of bread and best butter. Sometimes the shells wouldn't come off the eggs properly and there would be lumps out of the whites. If he was in a very bad mood he would get me up to cook some more eggs.

When I heard the front door bang shut I held my breath and waited. Usually I would hear him go into the kitchen and a short time later I would hear his bedroom door close, and then I would breathe a sigh of relief and be able to sleep. That night he didn't go into the kitchen; there was complete silence. After a while I crept out of my room to listen from the top of the stairs. I heard my Daddy crying, just as he had done when my real mother had left us five years before. He didn't hear me when I stole into the living room and I watched him for a minute. I couldn't bear it; I ran to him and threw my skinny arms around him. 'Daddy! Daddy, has Granddad died?' I couldn't think what else would make Dad cry like this. I had surprised him and he quickly wiped his face with his big white hanky, then he held me away from him.

'I'm so sorry, none of it is your fault, none of it. She shouldn't be taking it out on you. It was her own choice,' he said, looking at me squarely through watery eyes. I said nothing; he had a hair-trigger temper and I was afraid to spoil this very rare moment.

'Will I make you a cup of tea?' I asked him after he had stared into the fire for a few minutes. He nodded and when he had drained his cup he said gently, 'Go to bed now. It'll be all right.'

I was still wide awake long after I heard Dad shut his bedroom door. I knew he had been talking about Mam, but what was she taking out on me? I knew she hated me and until now I thought it was something I had done; there was something else, but what?

Dad wasn't home much after Granddad left; he went to the pub after work most nights and we hardly saw him. Mam worked long hours in the factory canteen. She took the boys to the company's Christmas party; I wasn't allowed to go. I didn't care. I waited until they were out of the street and sneaked out through the back entry, a long lane that ran along the back of the endless rows of terraces, and spent the rest of the day with a few of my school friends. We went to Shirley's house and they did my hair in a swishing ponytail and Shirley loaned me one of her dresses with yards of skirt and several 'paper nylon' underskirts along with a pair of her 'kitten heel' pumps; I felt like a princess. We jived in the living room to Cliff Richard, Little Richard and Bill Haley and his Comets. We sighed dramatically at the sad songs of the Everly Brothers; we giggled and gossiped over *The Bunty* girls' comic and drank milkshakes that Shirley's mam made for us. This was a warm and happy home with a young mother who tried to sing along with 'our' pop songs and a father who popped his head around the door to say hello and retreated. It struck me that the atmosphere stayed exactly the same as before he arrived home and Shirley merely turned her head in his direction with 'Hiya, Dad'.

Our Dad didn't allow pop music, dancing, modern clothes or friends in the house. In fact the only person to visit our house was an Irishman who brought us cheap cornflakes on Friday night; he worked in the Kellogg's factory at Trafford Park. One Friday he didn't arrive and the following week he told Dad that a man had fallen into the Rice Krispies barge and had been killed; the company had closed the factory for the day. The Irishman was annoyed because 'I lost a fughing day's pay.' He blessed himself and asked God to have mercy on the poor man's soul.

Dad thought that rock and roll and the fashions of the day were 'muck'; his idea of entertainment for us was to have us all seated against the wall of the living room on the kitchen chairs whilst he played a selection of classical music on the piano. Always the recital ended with his party piece, Liszt's Hungarian Rhapsody No. 2 in C minor. Dad never used the 'soft' pedal. Sometimes we had an even 'bigger treat' when he would walk around us with his old second-hand violin like a gypsy in a film, leaning towards one of us, putting so much feeling into 'La Paloma' or his particular favourite, 'Meditation'. We tried not to laugh at him; that would have earned us a stinging slap on the ear. When he finished each piece he would say through a satisfied sigh, 'Aah, your Da's a genius.'

Dad bought a state-of-the-art, seven-inch, reel-to-reel tape recorder for the ridiculously vast sum of £63, much to Mam's disgust and anger.

''Ow the 'ell do you expect us to pay for that bloody thing,' she inquired of Dad as she rolled a very thin cigarette from her tobacco jam-jar.

Dad told her not to worry – it was just seven and sixpence a week on the 'never never'; was that too much to ask for a working man to have a bit of pleasure?

Mam sighed as she drew deeply on the roll-up. 'It wouldn't be so bloody bad if you was a bloody working man,' she threw at him as she exhaled a cloud of smoke and as usual a blazing row followed. Mam appeared not to hear or listen as Dad ranted and raved; she stared passively ahead of her and noisily slurped tea from her pint pot.

Dad took his 'recording sessions' very seriously and even hid the clock under a cushion so that the microphone wouldn't catch the loud ticking; woe betide any of us who coughed or snuffled when he was recording. One day Dermot had terrible trouble trying not to snuffle and tried in vain to push the rivers back into his nose with the palm of his hand, completely unaware that Noel, Maurice and I were watching him from our chairs lined up on the opposite wall, our shoulders shaking with mirth as we tried to stay quiet. Of course we didn't realise that Dad could see this pantomime in the reflection of the piano panels until he exploded with anger and chased us upstairs swiping the back of our heads as he followed to the magical fourth step where he couldn't reach us. He never actually followed us up to the bedrooms and he couldn't reach us beyond the fourth step. He went back to his recording, telling us what a 'shower of fecking wasters' we were. The three of us were grateful to be spared the rest of the 'concert'.

Christmas was a miserable affair that year, apart from a dinner of roast chicken that Dad cooked; he always cooked the Christmas dinner. We of course did the cleaning up afterwards; we were always grateful that we didn't own too many pots and dishes. We had our present of a half crown each and were allowed to watch the television for a few hours through the day but otherwise it was just like any other day. There was no sense of festivity, no fun. We could hear the neighbours on either side greeting friends and family, and then loud conversations and laughter; every so often there would be happy shouts somewhere outside of 'Merry Christmas, love, ta ta'. Twinkling coloured fairy lights that took on a magical appearance when the glass steamed up lighted most of the little front windows, which reflected prettily on the wet, grey path, giving the street a cosy feel. Even old Mrs Atkinson, who lived across the road and spent every single day sitting on a chair just inside her open front door fighting for each painful breath as she chainsmoked her Woodbines, put a small Christmas tree with lights and silver tinsel in her window and had visitors who carried armfuls of pretty parcels into her house.

I thought about Granddad and my mother and prayed to Our Lady for them to have a happy time, and thought how for the first time that I could remember there was no Christmas pudding.

One cold February day when I came home from school Dad was sitting by a blazing fire.

'Hurry up, Ebbs, we've been waiting for you,' he said as I came into the living room on my way to the kitchen. My insides jerked and turned over and an icy finger of fear ran down my spine; something was terribly wrong: Dad was being too nice. A delicious smell of cooked food invaded my nostrils and when I went into the kitchen I found my brothers seated around the table eating platefuls of pork sausages and fluffy mashed potatoes with chopped onion through it and garden peas, not the tinned marrowfat variety that was our usual fare. I sat at the table. Dad took a plate of food off the top of a pan of boiling water and placed it in front of me, telling me that he had kept it warm for me. All I could manage by the way of thanks was a weak smile. I couldn't speak, my mouth had gone bone dry and my stomach was jumping with butterflies. Dad leaned casually on the door frame and lit a cigarette, chatting easily with the boys. My mind was a whirlpool of confusion as I picked at my food; what was going on? I looked at Dad's relaxed smiling face and instinct told me that he would drop a bombshell any minute. Maybe he was going to send us all back to the convents. When the meal was over he told us to leave the clearing up for a minute; he had something to tell us. We followed him into the living room and stood in a line in front of him, most of us looking down at our feet.

'Jessie has moved out,' Dad announced calmly. This was the first time I could remember him referring to Mam as Jessie to us. There was no anger, resentment or regret in his voice; it was a bald statement of fact, like 'It's raining today' or 'I need petrol for the car.' There was a stunned silence and our heads snapped up to stare at him, as he looked at each of us; we waited for more but he didn't give us any more. I looked at my brothers; their expressions were blank and I had no clue how they were taking the news. Would we all be going into some English industrial school? Were there industrial schools in England? Maybe we would be going back to Ireland and the convents he had fought so hard to get us out of four years ago. Kevin and Dermot spent many hours dreaming of their former life in the convent and praying to be sent back; the other boys just took each day as it came and stoically struggled through, hoping things wouldn't get worse. On the other hand I had decided that I would run away the first chance I got and look for my real mother.

I knew that my real mother would buy me the bra that I so desperately needed. All the girls in my class now wore one, their breasts imprisoned rigidly in place pointing straight out just inches under their chins; mine were embarrassingly swinging about under my gym slip and I hunched my shoulders in a vain attempt to hide them. Mam had told me that she couldn't afford the two shillings and eleven pence it would cost to buy one; nor could she afford another pair of navy-blue knickers even though the only pair, which I had to wear for PE, were full of darning patches and far too small for me.

My real mother would have told me that I wasn't going to die when I woke up one morning and found blood on my sheet and terrible pain in my stomach. I gave my little treasures – except my rosary beads, which would drape prettily over my joined hands as I lay serenely in my coffin – to my brothers, telling them that I wouldn't need them any more. I had to ask for them back when a teacher at school told me that I had 'started', although she didn't say what I had started, and assured me that I would live to be a very old woman. 'That's how we women are able to have babies,' she explained. I didn't want a baby and told her so; she smiled and told me to go back to my classroom.

My real mother would have told me how important it was to be very clean now that I was growing into a young lady. She would have bought sanitary towels for me, not given me an old pinny to tear into rags which had to be soaked in cold salted water and boiled in an old pan after use ready for the next time; I was always terrified my brothers would see them. My friends were far too polite to tell me that I was smelly, but when one of the teachers pushed me away from her in disgust I realised and burned with shame and humiliation, but I didn't know what to do about it. Mam wasn't interested and I could hardly ask Dad. I started washing the knickers every night in cold water, scrubbing them with the big bar of green household Fairy soap we used for washing ourselves, and hanging them over the chair in my room. They were often still sopping wet in the winter when I put them on the next morning. Mam said it was dangerous to wash my hair or have a bath when I had 'the curse'. She didn't elaborate and my brothers thought I had caught some terrible incurable disease. They gave me sidelong glances and avoided coming into any kind of contact with me. Kevin and Dermot all but blessed themselves when at mealtimes we were together at the kitchen table and they had to sit next to me. I found it very funny but couldn't tell them that I was only having my periods – such things were never discussed in our house. The boys hoped they wouldn't get 'the curse'. I told them that it was a girl thing and they shouldn't worry. 'It's something we women have to put up with,' I said, tossing my head and trying to look very grown-up.

We didn't ask Dad any questions about Mam's whereabouts or why she had left. She had left several times before but Dad had always managed to find her and bring her back almost before she was missed by us. She had tried to leave before we left Ireland and had just made it to the ferry.

Dad was telling us how things were going to be different now: 'If we all pull together we'll be fine.' Not that he had done much 'pulling' up till now, but that didn't matter to me. I had my old Daddy back and a feeling of great joy surged through me. The boys, whom Jessie had treated well, except Dermot that is, didn't say how they felt about her leaving and we all carried on with our usual routine.

The following week Dad got a job as a maintenance painter at the Kellogg's factory. His good humour had lasted and we were beginning to relax when he was about; when he was out we even risked putting on the television and watching *Top of the Pops* and *Z-Cars*. If we heard his car pulling up outside we would jump up, turn off the television and dive upstairs, pushing the younger ones ahead of us; he never caught us.

Dad seemed to enjoy working at the cornflakes factory; he would whistle merrily as he got ready to leave in the morning. He bought a real Harris tweed jacket that smelled of peat and

Old Spice aftershave lotion and would give us a few pennies
when he went out at night. 'Buy a few sweets and be good
until I come home,' he would say; no threats or warnings of
what to expect if things were not right when he came home,
as he used to make. We stopped fearing him.

At the end of his first week at work Dad gave me ten
shillings to 'buy yourself some necessities', meaning underwear. I flushed with pleasure and got through my housework
with lightning speed, hardly believing my good fortune.
Shirley and Kay came to the market with me and we spent
ages choosing a bra, a new pair of navy knickers and white
ankle socks, and the girls gave me some of their old summer
uniform gingham dresses. At last I felt equal to all the other
girls in my class; I couldn't wait to go to school on Monday
when, feeling very pretty in pink gingham, I threw my shoulders back and proudly displayed my newly pointed breasts,
captured and hoisted to within inches of my chin.

Dad had made friends with a lady who worked in the factory and one Saturday afternoon he took me to her house to
meet her. She made coffee and when I said I didn't like it Dad
ordered me to drink it and then told me to drink his as well. I
was about to protest when he gave me the familiar cold hard
look that said 'do it or else'. I drank both cups. I watched from
the doorway of the kitchen as this lady put on her make-up,
leaning over the kitchen sink. She was wearing a tight skirt
and high heels and on the top half of her body she had just a
beautiful lacy bra. She didn't say anything but glanced at me
now and then without smiling. After a few minutes she asked
me to go and wait in the living room while she got ready. She
called Dad into the kitchen and when he came out he took me
home; he was in a bad humour but not with me. I didn't see
that lady again.

Dad was still very strict with us and we all had a very
healthy respect for him, but we didn't dread coming home

from school each day wondering if we had done anything wrong or worse if we had forgotten to do something right. He had decorated all the rooms and painted a wonderful abstract design on the kitchen walls. In the bathroom he had painted a seascape with a flock of gulls on the ceiling. I remembered he had painted a jungle on the bathroom wall in our flat in Fatima Mansions all those years ago before our lives had been turned upside down. When he painted the windowsills outside to look like genuine marble, a lot of the neighbours paid him to do theirs also. He only charged them ten shillings and the same amount for graining the hall doors. He became very popular in the street and everyone respectfully called him 'Mr Doyle'.

My brothers and I ran errands for old Mrs Atkinson and she always gave us a copper or two. We missed her when she went to Blackpool for a week but she brought us a huge pile of pink and white minty rock. When Dad saw it he ordered me to take it back to 'that dirty oul' one'. I was mortified but this very kind lady understood. We still ran her errands but made sure Dad didn't find out. He didn't mind us going next door to Mr and Mrs Evans, an elderly couple from Wales. Their home was sparkling clean and full of shiny china ornaments and crisp, clean net curtains on the windows. They were both small and plump with snow-white hair, smiling rosy faces and funny singsong accents. Mr Evans had a short, carefully trimmed white beard and was an artist; he gave me a painting of the Welsh valley he had been born in nearly eighty years before. It was as pretty and green as Ireland and I hung it in my bedroom. I hadn't seen a green field since we had arrived in England, and often when the longing for my real mother overwhelmed me I would imagine us wondering along the banks of the river that ran through the beautiful valley in the painting.

As the weeks wore on I became a competent little housekeeper. I was delighted when Dad bought me a shiny new Hoover twin-tub washing machine. He spent nearly an hour explaining how to operate and clean it, even though a monkey would have grasped it within five minutes. It took every ounce of my self-control to look interested enough to humour him. I considered myself to be 'the lady of the house' and was as happy as any thirteen-year-old could be in the cir- cumstances. Dad of course was very much the 'master' of the house and sometimes a flash of the old bad temper would erupt without warning, reminding us painfully what he was still capable of.

FOUR

One morning early in May as I carried Dad's tea tray up to his
bedroom I thought I heard the wet hacking cough. I stopped
in the middle of the staircase and listened. No, I thought,
shaking my head, I must have been mistaken. All I could hear
were my brothers starting their daily chores. Noel was raking
out the ashes from the fire grate in the living room; Dad liked
the fire to be lit when he came downstairs on cold mornings.
The others were in the kitchen rattling the dishes, setting the
table for breakfast and talking at the tops of their voices. One
of them banged the back kitchen door as he went out to the
lavie at the bottom of the yard. No, I was hearing things.
Balancing the tray on one arm, I knocked at Dad's bedroom
door and waited a few seconds until I heard him say as usual,
'It's all right, come on in.'

Trying not to bang the tray on the door so as not to make
him jump and put him in a temper, I pushed it open and
entered the darkened room. There was no mistaking the
corvine-like figure sitting hunched forward in the bed smoking a cigarette. My senses froze and rooted me to the floor as I
stared in disbelief, my mind registering the gaudy multi-
coloured striped cardigan draped over her shoulders. Jessie
was back.

'Well! Don't just stand there looking stupid. Get your
Mammy her tea,' was all Dad said, lighting a cigarette. I wasn't
able to control my shaking hands and the crockery rattled as I
put the tray on the bedside table. Jessie said nothing. I glanced

at her as I turned to leave the room, but she just stared ahead and as she drew deeply on her cigarette gave no sign that she had noticed my presence.

Downstairs my brothers were seated around the kitchen table eating their cornflakes. I hardly saw them as I reached up to the shelf for the blue-and-white-striped pint mug. No, I thought, she's not having this, she can have a bloody cup like everyone else, and I let the mug fall on to the lino-covered stone floor; it smashed into a hundred small pieces.

'She's back,' I told the boys savagely through gritted teeth. 'One of you take a cup up to her,' I said to them, and I fled out into the back yard and locked myself in the lavie without waiting to see their reaction to the shattering news. How could Dad do this? I asked myself over and over again. Hadn't we been happy these last three months? Now I knew for sure that Our Lady had not come with me to England. I wasn't even sure that she had left the convent with me. Apart from begging her to make Granddad stay, I hadn't asked her for anything and had just hoped she would look after me; but Granddad was right, this was indeed an unholy godforsaken country. I reached inside my dress and took my rosary beads from around my neck. I stared at them for a minute, letting them ripple through my fingers as the Reverend Mother's words echoed in my head: she had said that the rosary beads would protect me and that Our Lady would always be with me; but they had failed me. I clutched the golden crucifix and said my last Hail Mary:

> Hail Mary full of grace.
> The Lord is with Thee
> Blessed art Thou among women …

I felt no comfort from my prayer and threw the beautiful beads down into the deep, dark hole at the bottom of the ancient toilet bowl. I pulled the long rusty chain that hung from the cistern above my head. I watched impassively as they were flushed by the great rush of water out of sight around the shallow bend of the bowl. Now it was just me on my own. I knew that somehow I would find my real mother and Granddad one day. I was never going to accept this woman as my mother, no matter what Dad said, and I decided that I wasn't going to even try to get her to like me. I felt defeated and angry and wept bitter tears. I never referred to her as Mam again; she became Jessie. I was defiant as I returned to the house to face what lay ahead.

Maybe it was the insolent way I looked at her, maybe it was something that had been said before she had left us; perhaps it was that I was as tall as she was – but whatever it was, an uneasy truce was wordlessly declared between Jessie and me. I made a point of not speaking to her directly if it was at all possible, and then only in short sharp sentences. When Dad was within earshot, with a cunning that was alien to me I was deferential and respectful to Jessie, but we both knew that war was not far away; it was just a matter of time and who would fire the first shot. I didn't have long to wait.

One day Dad called me to my bedroom. When I entered the room and saw my bed I was shocked. My legs felt as if they were about to give way under me as I stared in disbelief at the huge array of sweet wrappers, fish finger packets and Malteser boxes scattered on the thin bedsprings. My mattress had been rolled back and lay on the floor at the end of the narrow iron bed.

'Well, I hope you can explain this, you bloody little rip,' Dad roared.

I was in confusion and I couldn't speak. Where had all this come from and why was it there? But as I heard Jessie enter the room behind me there was no doubt in my mind who had put it there.

'I told you, Dessie, she's a bloody little thief.' There was a note of triumph in Jessie's voice as she handed me a bucket and the sweeping brush.

Since Jessie had come home Dad hadn't reverted to his old harsh self and sometimes he even had me singing while he played the piano. He had told Jessie that there was a good possibility that with the right training I would make a half-decent soprano; my music teacher at school had written to him and told him that I had 'a voice' and it would be a great pity if it were wasted. I was elated; I hoped to join Maurice, who was at the Northern School of Music.

But now he slapped me across my face, causing my ears to ring and little white lights to dance in front of my eyes. 'Well, you fecking little bitch, where did you get this lot from?' He was beside himself with rage.

I couldn't answer him. I tried to, but no sound came out of my mouth. The next slap sent me reeling across the room. As Jessie turned to go our eyes met and I saw fear in her mean pinched face. I endured his rage for a few more minutes but it felt like hours and at last he went downstairs. I could hear my brothers crying but I was unable to go and comfort them; I felt too weak to get up off the floor. At last I heard the front door slam as Dad left for the pub. I cleared the rubbish off the bedsprings and wondered why fish finger packets. I remade my bed and lay on top of it. My brothers came in one by one and I tried to tell them that I was all right, but my face was swelling up and the younger ones cried. Then I dozed off.

The light was snapped on and I nearly jumped out of my skin. For a second or two I couldn't remember why I was sore.

'There you are, love. Drink this and you'll feel better.' Jessie was walking towards me carrying a cup and saucer full of steaming tea. I said nothing as she handed me the brew.

'I don't want you to get in trouble wi' police, love, so I 'ad to tell your father.' Her tone was conciliatory and she started to leave the room.

'Jessie,' I said quietly. It was the first time that I had addressed her by her name and it surprised her. She started back towards the bed and opened her mouth to say something. The devil took a hold of my hand and I threw the cup and saucer straight at her head, covering her with the hot tea. The cup and saucer shattered on the bare wooden floor. As the tea dripped down through her black greasy hair and formed droplets on her face I looked at her with loathing. I knew that if she told my father what I'd just done he would surely kill me, but I didn't care. The two oldest boys burst into the room, with a look of horror on their faces that would have been comical in other circumstances. But I was amazed when Jessie told them, 'It's all right, go on downstairs. I've 'ad a little accident.' I heard them clattering down the stairs and cries of 'God, she's done it now!' and 'Dad will kill her'; but I knew now that Jessie wouldn't tell Dad. I also knew that I had won the first battle; but there would still be the war to finish and I knew that my chances of winning that were next to nothing.

A subtle change came over Jessie. She tried to get me involved in the daily banter between her and the boys, but I chose to remain remote from her. I didn't trust her and felt that I had to be on my guard against her; I realised how dangerous she could be.

When Dad was out she would regale us with fantastic stories of her exploits during the war. If she was to be believed she had almost single-handedly won the war and Churchill was a personal friend. Of course the Duke of Edinburgh fancied her but he had to put his duty before his personal feelings.

I laughed with the boys the night when, having told us that she had a false wooden big toe, we watched fascinated as she cut the ugly grizzled nail with her nail 'sithers' as she called them.

'Mam, if that's a wooden toe how does it grow a nail?' Maurice, the intelligent one, or the braver of us, inquired of her.

Her answer was her usual retort when she was not able to explain some of her more outrageous stories: 'I'll clat your bloody ear 'ole, you cheeky bugger.' She carried on with her pedicure, telling us that she had only one lung, as she had coughed the other one up the day she was born and 'nearly died', but her dead grandmother had miraculously saved her life and she could remember every second of that day.

For nearly ten months Dad didn't speak a word directly to me; he had been convinced that I was a thief and liar. If I was in the same room as him he would say to one of my brothers, 'Tell that one to get out of my sight' or whatever he wanted me to do. I was devastated by his attitude. I didn't get a chance to explain to him, and of course my musical education was over. I spent most of my time in the kitchen when he was home.

'Very soon, girls, you will all be going out into the big wide world.' As our headmistress gave our class the final 'you are grown-up now' lecture, a huge sadness enveloped me. School had become a haven from the relentless drudgery and misery at home. I was going to miss my friends so much and wondered what Dad had in mind for me when it came to getting a job. I was amazed that my friends were able to pick any job they wanted. They were talking about being comptometer operators, whatever they were, window dressers or nurses; one clown told us all she was going to find a millionaire and never work. Some of my class were staying on for another year. That would have been my dream.

My headmistress had called at our house one night to

implore Dad to let me stay on. As usual Jessie was sitting hunched forward with her knees apart drinking tea from her new pint mug and smoking a roll-up.

'Mr Doyle, Evelyn has the ability to achieve so much. You must reconsider,' I heard her tell him. I burned with shame and humiliation when I showed her into our bare, sparsely furnished living room that, although clean, reeked of cigarette smoke.

'What would she want an education for? Sure, she'll have half a dozen kids around her skirts before long.' Dad was quite definite about it; I was to leave school in December. I wouldn't be fifteen until January.

Mr Merrion was a kindly-looking man with a grey, shaggy moustache, a full head of thick grey, curly hair and smiling, china-blue eyes.

'Well, Evelyn, why do you want to work at Woolworth's?' I opened my mouth to tell him that I didn't particularly want to work in a shop; I wanted to work at the deaf school. I had met Perry a couple of months before on my way to school; it didn't matter to me that he was a deaf mute – all I knew was that he was kind and very handsome and carried my satchel right to the school gate. He didn't seem to mind that I was scruffy and a bit smelly. When he shyly held my hand for the first time I blushed deeply and wondered what he saw in me. Dad and Jessie had been telling me for the last couple of years that I was dirty, useless and a waste of time; I felt ugly and awkward and secretly thought that Perry must have been blind as well.

'She's a hard worker and won't give you any trouble, I'll see to that,' Dad was saying to the manager, hardly acknowledging the fact that I was sitting right beside him. As far as he was concerned I had no say in the matter of my career; he hadn't even asked me what I would like to work at.

*

'That'll be seven and six, love.' The hairdresser was noisily chewing gum and had puffed on Woodbines all through the terrifying process of perming my hair. Long thick wires carrying metal rods attached to the ceiling connected to the electricity had burned my hair to a frazzle and the smell of ammonia was overpowering for days afterwards. Dad had insisted that I had to look 'respectable'. 'I'm not having you running around with your hair looking like a bird's nest.' He was of course referring to the beehive hairdo that was fashionable in 1961, and which I would have preferred. My humiliation was complete when he told Jessie to give me one of her hairnets to contain the thick wild bush that was now growing out of my head.

What a sight I must have looked that first morning with my bare feet crammed into brown school sandals, an old-fashioned satin tea dress with huge pink roses that Jessie had found at a market stall, and the now too short grey coat that I had worn on my first day at school; but according to Dad at least I looked 'respectable', if not elegant.

Dad hustled me through the large double glass doors. The glamorous sales girls with beehive hairdos of varying height, some it seemed at least a foot tall, coal black lined eyes and pale, almost white, lipstick, and tottering about on six-inch stiletto heels, were already at their counters on the vast, brightly lit shop floor. They were taking down the dust sheets, filling the counter stock from large brown boxes and chatting and laughing with each other and the warehouse boys, who were filling huge waste baskets on wheels with discarded papers and empty boxes. As I felt them watching me fear clutched my throat and I fixed my gaze firmly on the polished tiled floor. Dad strode ahead, leading me deeper into this Aladdin's cavern, urging me to keep up and look smart about it. Maureen, the staff supervisor, told him that it was all right, he could go, and, yes, she would be sure to let him know if I gave her any trouble.

'Sweet Jesus! What century did he come out of?' she mused as she gave me my uniform, a snow-white overall with a big red 'W' on the breast pocket and a cute little white stiffly starched tiara-shaped cap also with a big 'W'.

'You're really quite a bonny lass,' she said as she made the ugly hairnet into a snood and perched the cap on the top of the frizz that had escaped, fixing it firmly in place with kirby grips she held between her teeth. My heart turned over with pleasure: no one had told me that since I was a little girl.

As Cliff Richard sang 'Bachelor Boy', Maureen led me to the biscuit counter and introduced me to Mrs Palmer, the counter supervisor. 'Show her the ropes, Duchess,' she said and winked at me as she bustled away across the shop floor.

'The Duchess' was a tall, willowy slim lady with dark, greying hair done up in a very chic French pleat. She smiled warmly as she welcomed me to her 'little world of bickies'; she glided rather than walked along the rows of glass-topped biscuit boxes as she introduced me to custard creams, fig rolls and garibaldis. She showed me the secret stash of broken biscuits that she kept for her 'old ladies'. 'We have our regulars, dear. You'll soon get to know them, poor darlings.'

Dad visited me several times that first day and ordered me to pull the hairnet right over my hair to my forehead. 'People don't want your hairs in the biscuits,' he said sharply.

Maureen told him that it would be impossible to wear the regulation cap properly and as far as she was concerned during the day I was in the employ of F.W. Woolworth. 'Of course, Mr Doyle, what Evelyn has to wear after hours is nothing to do with us, but while she's here she wears what we want her to wear and how we want her to wear it.' She stomped off, her face almost purple with rage. This was her territory and she was having no man telling her how to run her department or her girls what to do. I was grateful to her and loved her for standing up to Dad.

Mrs Palmer went to lunch, or dinner as it was called then, at half past eleven. 'It won't be too busy for you just now, dear. I'll be back at twelve.' She spoke with a refined, soft accent, not the harsh nasal tones of most people I had met in Manchester. She told me not to panic and I was alone on the thirty-foot-long counter.

I didn't panic then but when it was my turn to go to lunch I stood uncertainly at the staff canteen door wondering what to do. As I watched the other workers move along the servery in the canteen I noticed that they handed money over to a fat lady sitting at a till near the big tea urn. Dad had given me a half crown for dinner money and bus fare home, and I wondered if it would be enough.

'Hello, love, I'm Dorothy but you can call me Dot.' A doll-like, tiny woman with an enormous beehive hairdo had minced over to me, her stride restricted by the tight pencil skirt showing through her open overall, and held her hand out to me. I had seen her working on the sweet counter and thought she was cheeky and bad-tempered with her male customers, but they thought she was funny and left the shop smiling. She invited me to join her table. 'We're over there.'

I followed her, through the din of rattling crockery and cutlery, the loud buzz of conversation punctuated by the occasional raucous laugh and a thick haze of cigarette smoke, to a red Formica-topped table in the far corner of the canteen. One of the two girls already seated dragged a chair from a nearby table for me. The smell of delicious food permeated my nostrils but I said I wasn't hungry; I didn't want to risk not having enough money, so I settled for a mug of tea and an empire biscuit. The three girls at the table could easily have been Dot's sisters; they all had the same stacked-high beehive hairdo, thick Max Factor pancake make-up and pale powdery-looking lips outlined with a dark brown colour. They were furiously puffing on Woodbines and supping tea from plain white pot mugs; they used their empty dinner plates, which were pushed into the middle of the table, for ashtrays. They nodded their hellos and I listened as they gossiped.

"'E tried to put 'is 'and down me front,' Babs, the blonde and older of the trio said as she inhaled deeply on her cigarette. The other two shrieked as she continued, snorting smoke through her nostrils, ' "Bugger off, you," I told 'im, "don't touch what ye can't afford, I'm saving meself." ' For what I couldn't imagine. She sniffed, pursed her lips and crossed her arms under her breasts, pushing them further up towards her chin. She demanded of the others, 'What does 'e think I am? Cheap or somat?' The others agreed that all 't' lads' were the same. I hadn't a clue what they were talking about but I laughed when they did and nodded knowingly, hoping they would think I was as grown up as they were.

By Friday I was feeling a little more confident, although I was tired and my feet were swollen and sore. Dot and her friends were starting to pull my leg about my hair and clothes but I didn't mind; they were kind and I laughed with them. Dad had called only a couple of times into the shop to see if I was 'all right' but I was sure he was checking up on me.

Mr Toomy, the floorwalker, came round to each of us carrying a wire tray with all the little brown pay packets standing up in neat rows and dished them out as though he were bestowing a huge bounty on every one of us, like a priest administering communion. The younger shop girls made faces at him behind his back, but when he handed me my first pay packet I blushed and almost curtsied to him with gratitude.

When I got home Dad was sitting by the fire. I handed him my wages. I hadn't dared to open the envelope to check if the money was right; I didn't even know how much my wages were. It didn't occur to me that this was my money, for which I had worked hard for nine hours every day.

'Soon there'll be six little packets like this to keep your old dad in comfort,' he smiled at me, as he wrote my national insurance number on the base of a wooden ashtray that one of the boys had made at school. My brothers were all looking on, waiting to see how much of my pay I would get; I had promised them they would get a share.

'Here you are, Ebbs, you've earned it.' He handed me a ten-shilling note and put the rest in the inside pocket of his jacket. I thought he was joking. My wages were £3 10s and he had already made it clear that I would have to pay my own bus fares and dinner money from what he called my 'pocket money'. But I didn't dare argue with him, I would just have to make it stretch through the week. If I gave my brothers six-pence each that would leave me with seven and six, and as long as I was careful and maybe walked to work a couple of times I would have about two or three shillings to spend on myself.

One morning in late February the Duchess didn't show up and Maureen told me to take charge of the counter. 'You'll be all right, love. If you're not sure what to do just give me a shout.'

I was determined to manage. I would have walked on fire for her – she was so kind and gentle to me. She was what I imagined a real mammy would be like. Dad had given up coming into the shop: Maureen guarded me like a tiger and stood with her hands on her hips behind my counter until he went away. Not that she said anything to him, but he got the message. At home he called her 'that bloody oul' busybody'. What he actually didn't like was that a woman could get the better of him and he was powerless to retaliate.

Dad hadn't had a woman telling him what he could and could not do since his mammy had died when he was only thirteen years old. His view was that of most men of his generation and in particular Irishmen, who saw women as the servants of their husbands, there to do their bidding, raise the children, keep the home clean and have their dinner on the table on the dot when they arrived home, whether from work or the pub – although in our case it was my brothers and I who cleaned the house and cooked his food; and a woman had to be ready to service her husband's sexual needs as and when he wanted. However, although this was generally still the case in Ireland, resulting in the phenomenon of 'Irish twins', when women commonly had two babies within a year, as my real mother had, things were changing very rapidly in England. Women were beginning to assert themselves, demanding equal rights to men, earning their own money and having fun. Dad didn't like the way things were going at all. 'Those young ones look like prostitutes,' he would tut in disgust when he had been into the shop and seen the brazen way some of the girls looked at him. To my acute embarrassment some of them even 'fancied' him. One day when he had been 'visiting' me a couple of girls from the basement sales floor happened to see him. 'Who was that gorgeous man, Evy?' I looked around me wondering what they were talking about; I hadn't seen any man, let alone a gorgeous one. 'You mean my father?' I was incredulous as it dawned on me who they meant. How could anyone fancy my dad?

The Duchess didn't turn in for work the following three mornings. Maureen became concerned. 'This is not like her. I've never known her to miss work in the three years she's been here.' She was thinking out loud more than giving me information. The staff supervisor would never discuss another member of staff with anyone her junior, much less with some one as lowly as me. Dot, who worked on the confectionery counter and Babs, who had charge of the clocks and watches on the far side of the floor and who spent a considerable amount of her time leaning against the back wall of her counter gazing into space or closely examining her hands, helped me when it was very busy, but for the most part I was alone on the counter.

When I went for my afternoon tea break, Maureen was in the canteen surrounded by the other supervisors. She was sniffling into her little white lace-edged handkerchief. She called me over. My stomach did a somersault. Had I been sacked? The supervisors never had the girls at their table and I knew that something was wrong.

'Sit down lass.' Her eyes were red and watery. Her companions shuffled around the table to make room for me. 'Oh lass, it's the Duchess, she's dead.' For a minute I didn't think I had heard her properly and my mind didn't register the meaning of her words. 'She just sat there for all the world asleep. Oh God! I'll never forget it,' she sobbed into her hankie. During her lunch break Maureen had gone round to find out where she was and had seen her through a window, sitting on a chair. She had banged on the door for several minutes before realising that something was wrong. When the police arrived and broke into her home they found that she was dead. We learned later that she had died of hypothermia and had been dead for three or four days. I wondered how, in a supposedly 'civilised' society, a person could die of cold in her own home and how she could have lain dead without anyone knowing. All the staff contributed a shilling for a wreath; I did a quick sum and reflected how that shilling could have bought a few bags of coal that would have saved the life of a very sweet and gentle lady. Although I was angry with God, I prayed to Him to look after Mrs Palmer when she went to heaven, as I was sure she would do.

'Here, have a piece of chuggy.' Dot handed me a small white tablet of Beechnut chewing gum as we sat on the top deck of the bus on our way home from work one Friday evening. She had also offered me one of her Woodbines. I had coughed and spluttered and felt sick but I didn't want to look 'soft' in front of my new friends and persevered until I had smoked about half the cigarette. Dot and Babs laughed. 'Your Dad won't be able to smell the smoke on your breath,' Dot told me. I chewed the minty gum with relief, clearing the foul taste from my mouth.

About six of us 'Woolies' girls caught the bus at St Anne's Square after work, running up the stairs and bagging the back seats before the posh Marks & Spencer girls got on at the next stop. 'Stuck up cows,' Babs would say, loudly enough for them to hear, but they ignored us. I enjoyed these half-hour journeys; they were the total extent of my social life. I took to walking to work a few times a week so that I could afford the ninepence for my five Woodbines and once a month I was able to splash out three and six for a bottle of Evening in Paris scent; calling it perfume would have been an insult to Coty's L'amante or Tweed; Chanel was another universe which I could never imagine inhabiting. The girls tried to persuade me to let them put my hair up in a beehive, but I was too scared that Dad would come into the shop; besides, it would have been impossible to comb it down, as the style required a huge amount of backcombing and Bel Air hairspray from a plastic bottle, which had to be squeezed hard for an even spray and set the hair like concrete. How I envied my friends and their carefree lives. I felt ugly and gauche beside them; I couldn't wait to get away from home, when I would be able to have tight jeans and a beehive and Max Factor damask rose lipstick. Maureen had told me that I could leave home when I was sixteen and Dad couldn't make me go back – that was the law in England. I would be sixteen in seven months' time and then I would be off to find my real mother and Granddad and start living my life. I dreamed of the day that seemed so far off.

'You can stay with me if you like now that my daughter is married,' Maureen offered. I pictured her cosy home with a warm fire and big soft sofa where I wouldn't be roared at or slapped about for the slightest thing. Probably I would be able to stay up after eight o'clock and watch television or go to the local youth club, where I would jive to Elvis and Bill Haley and his Comets, and eat fish and chips out of newspaper as I walked home with my friends. I really did believe this dream would come true and it kept me going through the hardest times.

FIVE

With Jessie and me both working bringing home about £8 a week between us, Dad didn't see why he should bother working. He had his unemployment money and he earned his 'beer' money playing the piano in the pubs around Manchester. Sometimes he would keep one of the boys away from school just so that they could make his meals, light the fire and clean the house. He was becoming remote again and his attitude to us became that of the notorious Irish Christian Brothers he loathed so much; we were nonentities there to do his bidding and make his life as comfortable as possible. My little brothers were starting to look like ragamuffins, new clothes being as scarce as hens' teeth, and their pale and pinched faces looked frightened whenever they were in Dad's company, as they were often the brunt of his bad temper when he woke up in the morning after he'd had a 'bad bottle'.

The house was constantly cold and damp, the fire only being lit in the living room when he was home, and often in the winter we would scrape ice from the inside of our bedroom windows. Food at home was a joke: tea was always three slices of bread and margarine with a scraping of mixed fruit jam that Jessie brought home from the jam factory, and at weekends it was a sausage sliced down lengthways to look like two sausages, with boiled potatoes and huge hard marrowfat peas. Dad had devised this menu when he learned one night of Jessie's attempt to put some variety into our diet by making stews with neck of lamb and using up the peelings from his boiled carrots. Dad wouldn't eat anything as lowly as stew or mutton. According to him that was 'peasant food' and not fit for a working man. He blew his top at Jessie and bawled at the top of his voice at her, 'In future they will have sausages, potatoes and peas, do you hear me?' He emphasised each word, striking the first three fingers of his left hand with his right index finger as though he was ticking off a shopping list. Jessie took him at his word and sausages, potatoes and peas became the menu for every weekend dinner. Thankfully the boys had school meals and I could buy a meal at work a few times a week; but none of us ever got fat.

However, neither Dad nor anyone else could break our spirits. More often than not we would all be upstairs or in the kitchen making fun of one of Dad's more outrageous outbursts. Some of my brothers could do a remarkable 'Dessie' impression: ' "Go on! Get out of me sight ya feckin' gobshites," ' Maurice would roar, holding his arms rigidly by his sides, fists clenched, doing a little jump *à la* Dad. He could do an amazing Dublin accent and we would rock with laughter. On Sunday mornings when we had finished our breakfast we would sit at the kitchen table singing cowboy songs; the boys would practise their harmonies with each other until Dad banged on the bedroom floor with his shoe, shouting at us to shut up. 'You sound like a bunch of shagging banshees.' But deep down we still loved Dad. I discovered many years later that the more abusive parents are to their children the more the children cling on. Baffling though it may seem, I understood that. I desperately wanted Dad to be my daddy again, as he had been before my mother had left us. I would sit on my daddy's knee and tell him about my busy day at school. My daddy used to brush my hair and neatly plait it every morning. When he came home from work he would listen proudly when I showed off my new reading skills. For my First Communion Day he made sure that I had the prettiest dress and splashed out a whole week's pay on a green coat with a real velvet collar and a matching velvet 'jockey' type hat, from no less a place than Clery's in O'Connell Street. I only wore the outfit that day; the following Monday it found itself languishing for ever in Brereton's pawnshop at Capel Street. Mammy wasn't allowed to come when he took me, as was the custom in Ireland, to visit all our relatives and his friends (but not Granny in Dùn Laoghaire or my real mother's sisters).

My younger brothers couldn't imagine Dad being any different from how he was; they didn't remember how much he loved us in those days. They didn't remember how he and Granddad made wooden forts and go-carts for us to play on, or how he would gather us all around the fire and tell us stories, or the fun we used to have at the Strawberry Beds when he took us fishing, or rabbiting in the Phoenix Park with his very smelly ferret which he carried in an old potato sack. We were so proud when he bought an old sewing machine and made green corduroy blouson jackets for us all. How concerned and frightened he had been when he had found one of the boys sitting on his hunkers at the edge of the canal peering deep into the murky water, in a gale so strong that he was not able to ride his bike. Daddy never smacked us and always had a smile and a cuddle for us all when he came home from work. Now my younger brothers shuddered at the thought of cuddles; they had never had any loving hugs that they could remember; they had only had their physical needs attended to by nuns who could not, because of the sheer number of boys, show affection. But the older boys grieved for the loss of a daddy who had been their hero and 'pal'.

One night when he had a temporary job driving a Mother's Pride bread lorry Dad was more than four hours late coming home and there were blizzards sweeping the country. We were all in tears as we frantically searched the house for a couple of pennies to call the company from a phone box, and there was a feeling of relief and security when he eventually came home. He never knew that all my brothers were sitting up in their bedroom and refused to go to bed until he was safely home.

'You have to take your holidays,' Maureen told me when I said I didn't need any. I preferred to stay out of the house, knowing that if I was at home I would be Dad's servant. I wouldn't have minded that too much, but his bad temper frightened me. I had started to shake uncontrollably when he shouted at me, and when he slapped me around the head or punched me in the back I would tremble for hours afterwards and fervently wish to be dead. Jessie never tired of telling him how dirty I was, how lazy and sly I was and how I would never amount to anything. 'You mark my words, Dessie, she's trouble that one is.' But I ignored her and now that I was working, days would go by when I wouldn't even see her.

When Maureen told me I had to take time off, I left work on the Friday night feeling really miserable; but when I told Dad that I had two weeks off he told me to find a job to fill in. I couldn't have been more pleased.

'I'm on the change,' Jessie told me. I couldn't imagine what she was 'changing into' but she had developed dark circles under her eyes and her skin was a dirty ash colour. For a brief moment I felt pity for her; she looked so tired and ill. 'Run to the herbalist shop on your way home from work and get two penn'orth of pennyroyal.' She didn't often ask me to do anything for her because I would always find an excuse not to do what she asked of me, but this time I relented, even though it would mean missing my dinner break. I had got a job waiting on tables at the UCP Restaurant for the two weeks of my imposed summer break during Manchester 'Wakes' fortnight. There to my utter amazement people actually ate cowheels and tripe, which is what the restaurant specialised in; I wouldn't have been surprised to see sheep heads being served up. But there were also stews and homemade meat and 'tater' pies, steamed treacle pudding and apple turnovers. I was grateful when at the end of the day the supervisor would share out any leftover food between the staff to take home. My brothers would be waiting eagerly for my arrival home to see what goodies I had in the big shopping bag I took to work.

SIX

'Start packing, Jess.' Dad was in a great mood, happy and optimistic. He had found a house in the country.

I said a sad goodbye to my friends at Woolworth's. Dad ordered me to leave. 'It's too far and too expensive to travel all the way to Manchester from where we're going. Hand in your notice.' He was right, of course.

Maureen hugged me tight and told me that if I ever needed her she would always be there for me. I was embarrassed by this display of affection but felt a warm glow of happiness that someone valued me and would miss me. I said I would write and thanked her shyly for her kindness to me.

'Ta-ra, love,' the girls shouted after me as I jumped off the bus for the last time. I stood on the pavement waving to my friends as they knelt on the back seat of the bus until it disappeared from sight and was lost in the traffic of Stretford Road.

Greenfield was one of a cluster of five villages clinging to the west side of the cold windswept and bleak Pennine Moors and if there was beauty in my new surroundings, I failed to notice it. The day after we arrived in the village Dad drove me to the mill.

When we left the weaving shed, without a trace of irony Dad commented, 'Jasus! You wouldn't get me working in there for any money.' The rhythmic clickety-clack noise of two hundred belt-driven looms was frightening and overwhelming and we were deaf for a minute or two after we left;

dust and fluff created by the constant movement of wool filled the huge shed with a thick haze. The weavers patrolled their looms, eyes glued to the brightly coloured cloths as they inched out along the front of the looms, forming a beautiful patchwork that seemed so inappropriate in such a hellish place. Occasionally a coarse cry would cut through the din as the workers attracted each other's attention and they would conduct a conversation in their own highly developed sign language accompanied by exaggerated lip movements. There were no beehives or black-lined eyes here that I could see. Most of the women had their hair in rollers hidden under headscarves; large aprons with pockets in the front covered old skirts and cardigans. Some of them had their stockings rolled down to their ankles; the rest of them were bare legged. The men wore navy-blue overalls and most of them clattered up and down on the duckboards between the looms, their feet clad in wooden clogs.

Yet again Dad had made up his mind about where I should work. 'They pay good wages.' He was matter of fact about it; there was no point in my arguing with him.

On my first morning the personnel manager introduced me to the foreman, a tall extremely thin man whose humourless face was varying shades of reds and purple. 'This in Mr Higginbottom, Evelyn,' Miss Whitehead told me.

He strode ahead of me towards the back of the weaving shed and after a brief conversation with the weaver left me with a curt nod. I got off on the wrong foot with Mr Higginbottom: I thought Miss Whitehead was joking – I had never heard such a name and burst out laughing. Neither of them was amused. I blushed and apologised, biting my bottom lip in a desperate bid to stifle the laughter. Mr Higginbottom ungraciously brushed my apologies aside and told me to follow him.

My fellow workers were blunt and abrupt and as they were

paid 'piecework' they had their noses to the grindstone from clocking on to the end of the day. I felt awkward and very young. At dinner time an eerie silence descended on the shed when the main belt was switched off and the weavers sat at the end of their looms reading and eating their sandwiches in silence. Every loom was switched on the instant the main belt was turned on again a half hour later; there was no sauntering back to work with obvious reluctance, as at Woolworth's: these people made their own money and squeezed every shuttle 'pic' that was humanly possible from the loom during their eight-hour shift.

But an old hand called Ambrose was infinitely patient as he trained me to weave and to tie knots at lightning speed when the warp was shredded by a broken shuttle. Soon I was allowed to run my own four looms. Noel joined me when he left school later that year, and we formed a great working team as we helped each other to keep the looms going through breakdowns and toilet breaks. Dad was delighted with our wages. Some weeks we could earn £13 each and he would give us a 'bonus' of £1 extra.

Dad got a contract to decorate a group of pubs from the local brewery, taking on Maurice as his apprentice. Life could have been so good at this point, but with all this extra money flowing in, Dad took up the life of a country squire. He brought home an adorable little cocker spaniel puppy and bought himself a rifle. He took to driving around in his new pale blue Hillman Minx estate car wearing his Harris tweed jacket and became a familiar figure in the village.

It was the dog that did it, and in particular the yellow sulphur powder the chemist recommended as he didn't have the ointment the vet prescribed for the dog's perpetual sore ears. Dad went berserk at me when I handed over the small tin of powder. He roared at me that I was a stupid bitch and what harm did the 'poor little fella' do to me to be so spiteful – on and on he went. He wouldn't let me explain that the 'sulphur' was not, as he thought, just for making gunpowder and matches, but was also commonly used for treating skin diseases. As he ranted and raved at me I decided that the time had come to run away and find my real mother.

The spaniel became the prince of the house. Often, after a hard day at the mill, Noel and I were made to sit on hard kitchen chairs if the dog required the small sofa to sleep on. I was extremely jealous of Moghill Max Wellington III, or Sailor to use his common name. Dad poured all his love and affection on that bloody mutt, who got the best steak mince, chicken and liver and was never shouted at; whatever he did was always our fault, be it chewing shoes, shitting under Dad's bed or limping, which he quickly learned would get him carried home from the long walks Dad insisted my brothers took him on, starting at six in the morning. The dog became the centre of all attention in the house.

Margaret said, 'He'll never find you. I promise not to tell anyone, honest.' She was the only other young girl in the shed and we had become firm friends. She combed my hair every morning into a much-desired beehive and let me help myself to her make-up bag before we went out to our looms. I had confided to Margaret my plan to run away and she insisted that she would help me. To her it was a very exciting, romantic adventure with me as the tragic heroine; I don't think she was able to comprehend the fear that I felt. She lived with her widowed mother in a small village three or four miles further towards Manchester. Her mother had agreed to put me up for a couple of days, unaware that I was 'running away'.

The urgent knocking on the door annoyed me and I tried to ignore it. I had just put my hair up in Margaret's rollers and was in the middle of smearing Max Factor pancake make-up on my face. Elvis was loudly 'itching like a man in a fuzzy tree'. I lit a Woodbine and I opened the door. Before I knew what was happening Dad's large hand yanked me out of the house. I screamed and kicked out with my bare feet but he was too strong for me to break free. People were staring but no one intervened, although I cried out for someone to help me. I knew I would get the hiding of my life when he got me back home. He had parked his car at the bottom of the street and by the time he threw me on to the back seat my feet were bleeding from the rough cobbles.

Dad had got Mr Higginbottom to threaten Margaret with the sack if she didn't tell them where I was. Telephones were a long way away for ordinary working people and she had no way of warning me that I was to get a surprise visitor.

'Where did you think you were going?' he asked when we got home. To my amazement he wasn't shouting; he seemed hurt and upset that I would want to leave home and his 'protection'. I told him that I was going to find my real mother. Tears rolled down his face as he told me, 'Your mother is dead, so you can forget her.' I instinctively knew he was lying and told him so.

Something strange happened to me that day. I had no fear of Dad, and I boldly flounced out of the room, slamming the door after me. Dermot was sitting on the bottom of the stairs, his eyes huge in his frightened little face, his hands clasped tightly between his knees. I touched his shoulder and felt him trembling. My little brother's fear brought my temper to boiling point. Hadn't I had to care for all my brothers since they were born and here I was letting them live in misery because I wasn't brave enough to fight their corner. Well, today I had nothing to lose. I went back into the living room. 'You're a bully and a coward. I hate you and I detest her.' There was no stopping me. I screamed at my father, 'He,' I pointed to

Dermot through the open door, 'in fact, we all, would have been better off if you had just left us in the schools. Why didn't you just go away? What did you bother coming back for?' I had gone too far. I knew it as I spat the words at him, so it came as no surprise to me when he jumped out of his chair and slapped me about the face several times.

Later that night, as I lay in bed shivering with cold and terrified at the force of the temper I had displayed earlier without any thought of the possible consequences, I resolved to plan my escape more carefully.

It was more difficult than I had imagined and it was not until a year later that my chance came. Dad persuaded Jessie to get a job at the mill so that she could keep an eye on me. She was a diligent warder, watching me like a hawk at work, but I made sure that she had nothing to report to Dad. Sometimes she tried to provoke me but I turned her barbs into jokes. I had naively thought that we could at least be civilised towards one another at work, but she would insist on embarrassing me in front of our fellow workers.

Ambrose, my trainer, told her through a cloud of fragrant pipe tobacco smoke, 'Leave t' lass alone, Mrs Doyle. Perhaps if she were th' own kiddie ...' he trailed off as Jessie jumped up from the bench and ran to the toilets.

I followed her. I felt some sort of misguided loyalty towards her and I knew she was upset. 'Don't worry about it, it doesn't matter,' I told her. When she looked at me I saw pain in her eyes and for a split second I wanted to hold her and give her some comfort. I had begun to realise that her life with Dad was no bed of roses, but surely she couldn't be blaming me for that. If only she would talk to me. 'Couldn't we try and get on?'

She shook her head as I handed her a wet paper towel to wipe her tear-stained face. I was concerned; Jessie never cried, even when she and Dad were having the most violent rows.

Not that he ever hit her – she would not have put up with that.

I could have sworn that there was gratitude in her expression; but maybe it was just wishful thinking on my part. I knew that if she lived to be a hundred Jessie would never be able to like me and if I was truthful I didn't suppose I would ever be her best friend. Nevertheless, whilst we didn't exactly become friends, a new understanding was forged between us, but she still wouldn't tell me where she disappeared to from time to time. We had all assumed that she had been going to see her mother in Yorkshire, but she still went off even after her mother died.

I remember one time when Jessie had been there for me, on my first ever date. One of my pals at the mill had arranged a blind date for me, thinking that my father would never allow me to go out. To my surprise he heard about it from one of my brothers. It was just after I had run away and he was trying to show me that home was the best place for me and that he was a 'great da' after all. 'It's time you started going out occasionally,' he said. I was utterly embarrassed but delighted when he took me to Cheetham Hill, where all the Jewish garment manufacturers sold clothes very cheaply. I chose a cute little powder blue suit in bouclé wool with a box jacket and a pair of cream kitten-heel shoes. I felt very grown-up and 'with it'. Dad's budget didn't run to a pair of stockings, but never mind, I was happy. Jessie insisted that I bring the boy home for tea before we went off to the cinema.

I waited at the bus stop in the deserted main street in the pouring rain and shivered with cold. I was about to give up when an amazing sight approached me. Oh no! It was a boy who was considered the village idiot and the butt of many jokes. He was dressed like a tramp and had holes in the elbows of his very dirty jersey; his greasy hair was hanging down past his collar. I was mortified. Wondering whether to run, I glanced across the street to the Conservative Club and saw Dad watching me through the window, pint in hand and laughing fit to burst. I pulled a face at him. I took Frankie back to the house. Jessie had laid the table with a white tablecloth and a spread of ham salad, bread and butter and cakes.

"Ey, you lot, get up them bloody stairs,' she shouted at my brothers, jerking her thumb in the direction of the staircase. They all burst out laughing when they saw who I had brought home. My brothers knew him and apparently he was very popular with all the boys in the village, but had never been known to have a girlfriend. In the kitchen, I was almost in tears and asked Jessie to send him away.

"E's a rough diamond, love,' she told me, and insisted that I should go ahead with the date. Cringing with shame and embarrassment I dumped him at the cinema when he went to get ice cream.

On my seventeenth birthday the boys presented me with a quarter-pound box of Maltesers. I was touched and very proud that they had saved up the one shilling and sixpence just for me. Dermot said, 'When I am grown up I am going to buy you the bestest dress in the whole world.' I choked back tears. I wanted to hug him, but that was not part of what we did; we only knew how to show our love for each other by being there and helping each other when needed. I often waited at the back door for the youngest ones as they came home from school, ready with a wet rag to wipe dirty knees and a shoe brush to clean muddy shoes – these were cardinal sins according to Dad. He had forgotten what it was like to be a small boy. He would never have tolerated the boys behaving as he had done, mitching from school to go fishing and rabbiting with his pals; nor would he put up with any 'backchat' as he called it; he had to be obeyed without question. However, he had been a little easier over the last few months and even laughed with us occasionally.

I hadn't expected a birthday present from Dad, and was stunned when, after breakfast he beamed at me, 'Happy birthday, Ebbs,' and pulled out a large box about four feet tall and twelve inches wide, from the cupboard under the stairs. I had a few seconds to imagine what was in the box – a bike perhaps? I had begged him to let me have a Lambretta scooter like the other girls in the village, but to no avail. Still, a bike would be wonderful: that long walk to the mill at half past five on icy cold Pennine mornings used up precious energy I needed for the hard shift ahead of me. It couldn't be anything else but a bike I was sure. I was so excited; Dad wasn't so bad after all! My brothers all gathered round as I stripped off the brown tape and tore the top of the box.

'Thank you, Dad, it's what I've always wanted.' I tried to keep the sarcasm out of my voice. My brothers hurriedly scattered from the living room. It was a 'Z' bed, with a headboard that formed a narrow table-top when it was folded.

'It'll add a little bit of extra furniture to your room,' Dad enthused, 'and now you have a place to put your statue.' He had given me a very large green chalk figure of a dancer holding out her skirt some time before when he had been decorating an old lady's house. It was the only ornament in my otherwise bare room.

I set about my housework crushed with disappointment. As my spirits had soared for the few seconds before I had opened the box, I had felt that surely this was the beginning of a new peace between Dad and me. Whatever had been going through his mind when he had decided on the present God only knew. It wasn't as if I was allowed to have friends staying and we never had visitors. Maybe Granddad was coming back. I held on to this thought as I attacked the onion for Dad's lunch before I got ready for my back shift. I carefully peeled and washed one half and put the other in the string bag that hung behind the kitchen door. I put his meal of fried mince-meat, onions and mashed potatoes on a tray and was about to take it to him in the living room. I didn't know he was behind me until I felt the slap on the back of my head.

'Yar dirty little rip, ye,' he roared at me. He accused me of not having washed the onion before I had cooked it.

I yelled back at him that I had washed it, but he wouldn't be convinced. I tried to run out of the back door as the plate of food flew past my head and crashed on to the wall; I watched as the food slid slowly down the wall towards the newly painted skirting board and finally formed a disgusting mound on the floor.

After I had made him another meal I stuffed my only 'good' pair of knickers and a tin of baked beans into my hand-bag and left for work. I managed to get through my shift and was relieved when Jessie left the mill at six o'clock without noticing that I was in a state of panic and fear. I had no inten-tion of going home ever again, but this time I told no one.

My heartbeats were so loud that I really believed that they would be heard outside as later that evening I stood on the toilet bowl of the ladies' public toilets in the village square. It was pitch dark and eerie; I could hear little feet scurrying around beneath me as I watched Dad cruising around the vil-lage in his Hillman Minx estate car, obviously searching for me. When he passed close to the toilets I held my breath and beads of cold sweat dribbled down the small of my back. I could see his face; he didn't look too angry but you could never tell with Dad. He looked concerned, though. His expression took me back to my childhood when at six years old I developed scarlet fever and was sent to hospital, and he would peer anxiously into each open hatch through which visitors were allowed to see loved ones. Then I would be shouting, 'Daddy here I am,' but not tonight.

At last he appeared to give up his search and turned the car in the direction of the road we lived on. I sat on the seat and waited for what seemed like hours before I ventured out into the darkness. I prayed that Mr Dyson, our local bobby, wouldn't be patrolling on his little Honda 50 moped. Keeping as close to the buildings as possible, I made my way out of the village up on to the main road that led to Manchester and freedom.

I had less than ten shillings in my purse when I boarded the late night bus that ran between Huddersfield and Manchester. I was dismayed when the conductor asked for three and sixpence for a ticket to the terminus at St Anne's Square, but I wanted to get as far away as possible, to reduce the chances of Dad finding me. As the bus headed into the city centre through a suburb I noticed a convent and jumped off the bus at the next stop. The Reverend Mother at my old convent had told me that there would always be a welcome for me in God's houses.

The nun said, 'Of course you may stay for tonight, but unless you have employment it will be only for tonight.' Nightmares haunted me that night as I lay on a narrow iron bed in a tiny, whitewashed room. The only decoration was a large crucifix of Christ dying. There was far too much blood for my liking on that particular cross and I tried not to look at it. Again I held the baby that fell to bits in my arms, but this time I was trying to run away from a giant blue devil and I dropped the baby on the steps. I wanted to go back and pick it up but I was afraid; the devil picked up the baby.

The next day I went to see the Reverend Mother. She had the newspaper open at the situations vacant page. 'What would you like to work at?' I hadn't thought about that so I asked her for suggestions. She thought that a temporary job working as a mothers' help would do until I could decide on a career. She circled an advertisement and gave me directions to an address near by.

When I got there I stood waiting for the 'lady' of the house to finish her conversation on a white telephone. The house was a mansion, beautifully furnished, and a thick pale cream carpet covered all the floors that I could see. A lovely dark-eyed girl, not much older than me, asked the little boy who was playing at his mother's feet what he would like to eat.

'Beans on toast,' he said. I noted that he didn't say 'please' and I thought he was very rude to the girl; he was quite a cross-looking child. His mother, glamorous in skin-tight, white trousers and a deep pink, fluffy sweater, continued her conversation, completely ignoring me and anything else that was happening in the room.

The *au pair* returned with the food for the child but he must have changed his mind. I watched horrified as he took the plate off the tray and emptied the contents on the cream carpet.

'For goodness sake, Maria, get the child what he wants, and clean up that mess,' the mother interrupted her conversation to shout at the girl.

'Excuse me,' I said. I couldn't let the girl get into trouble with her employer and I was angry that a child could behave in that manner and get away with it. 'The little fella asked for beans on toast and what he actually wants is a good slap on the legs.'

She ordered me out of her house immediately and obviously used her white telephone to call the Reverend Mother, for when I got back to the convent she said that she didn't think I would 'fit' in and it would be best to make other arrangements.

I stood at the bus stop wondering what to do and where I could go. I was very hungry but my total assets amounted to four and ten pence and that wasn't going to take me far. I decided to risk calling Mr Rhodes at the mill. I asked him if he would not give my wages to Jessie as I had left home. His sympathy towards me made me cry and I sobbed down the telephone that I was sorry to have just walked out and I hoped he would give me a reference. As the rapid pips in the earpiece told me that my tuppence was nearly up I just about heard Mr Rhodes telling me to come and see him.

I trusted Mr Rhodes, who was a great grandson, a few times removed, of Cecil Rhodes who founded Rhodesia, and a benevolent boss well used to dealing with the 'bloody' peasants. He'd had a big row with Dad once. I had been sent home with appalling period pain but when Jessie told Dad that I was 'play acting' to get attention, Dad sent me back to work. Twice more that day after Mr Rhodes had told me to go home Dad sent me back to work. Mr Rhodes' office had a large glass window that overlooked the weaving shed and he saw that I was clearly not well. Finally he took me home himself in his huge black Humber Hawk and told Dad in his best cut-glass, educated 'I am the boss' voice that he would get the NSPCC to him if he didn't take more care of me and further he noticed how ill-kempt and undernourished I was. 'How do you expect the girl to do a hard day's work, and believe me it is a hard day's work, if she is ill fed and as neglected as your daughter appears to be?' He instructed Dad not to send me back to work for at least two more days and stalked down the garden path. Dad was pale with rage and humiliation and called Mr Rhodes a 'fecking stuck up bastard Englishman'.

Now I went back to see Mr Rhodes. He told me that if ever I needed help to be sure and let him know; and he handed me a fat pay envelope with £23 17s 6d, along with my cards. I was rich.

SEVEN

The landlady showed me the room.

'It's £3 10s a week and one week in advance.' She was about four foot six inches tall and had a large hump on her back, but her face was pretty, although hard and uncompromising.

'I don't normally take Irish, so take care or you'll be out on your arse in a flash,' her harsh voice rasped at me.

I just nodded agreement. I had no choice but to take the room in the stinking, rundown, red-brick terrace in the poorest part of Oldham. It was the cheapest I could find, having searched for hours and having been turned away by some landlords and landladies who had notices on their windows saying 'NO BLACKS OR IRISH'.

That night on my way up the stairs I almost crashed into a tough-looking man dressed all in black and with a vivid pink towel slung around his neck. I averted my eyes, mumbled an apology and fled to my room, locking it behind me. I felt a little safer when I had pushed the heavy dressing table against the door. I had just met the man to whom I would be married for more than twenty years and he had scared me witless.

One evening I decided to go to my room because the smell of the fish and chips the other lodgers were eating from newspaper was making my mouth water. As usual I had spent the majority of my wages over the weekend, not sparing a thought for the week ahead.

I was in the second month of my new independence and most of the time I was broke and hungry, and at times I was very lonely. I felt strangely adrift, having no one to tell me what to do; who did I ask for permission to go out at night and who was I scared of if I was late? For several weeks after I had left home an acute sense of fear overcame me when I opened my wage packets: how could this be my money? I had become 'institutionalised' over the last six years from constant criticism and being told that I was useless, and from never in any way being able to assert my individuality, in the same way that long-term inmates of industrial schools, psychiatric hospitals or prisons were when they ceased to be able to make decisions for themselves and had to comply to rigid rules or risk punishment. I had no confidence in myself as an individual. And I was suffering from being without my 'tribe'. I so wanted to see my brothers; and yes, I even missed Dad at times.

I had been able to walk straight into a job in one of the many cotton mills dotted around the town. Oldham, like many northern towns, was full of the huge, ugly, red brick square buildings, each with its own tall chimney. Along with the coal fires from the endless rows of terrace houses, they belched out smoke day and night, covering everything with black grime and filling the air with suffocating dirty yellow fog in winter. Brave little hydrangea bushes covered in traffic dirt struggled to grow on tiny squares of front gardens on the better-kept streets of this dismal town, which couldn't have changed much since Blake asked if Jesus would have lived amongst 'those dark satanic mills'; given the choice, He probably wouldn't have.

Not many young girls wanted to go into the mills in the early sixties. They wanted glamorous jobs as secretaries, hairdressers or nurses. They had seen their mothers and aunties grow old before their time, worn out and breathless from hard toil in the cotton mills, and they were having none of it. Further education was now available to almost everyone.

Families were smaller in England than they were in Ireland and children were not required to earn a wage to supplement the family income the very second they became old enough to go out and work. The mass unemployment of the past was gone. But I wasn't concerned with any of this; my main goal in life at the time was to survive in a frightening world without the support of family or friends.

Most of the lodgers in the house were rough, working men, unkempt and foul mouthed, and I was the only girl apart from Betty the landlady. As the weeks rolled on I noticed that almost all the lodgers had a healthy respect for the man I had seen on the stairs that first night. They would relinquish the only armchair in the residents' lounge when he came down to watch the television. He never said much and seemed not to notice anything that was going on around him. No one got close to him and I tried to avoid him.

Now as I waited in my room until the men had finished eating, the hunger pangs gnawing painfully in my stomach, I comforted myself that tomorrow was pay day and planned what I would eat. I had only been able to afford a pint of milk by way of food over the previous two days. I hardly heard the soft tapping on my door. My heart turned over with fright; no one ever came to my door.

'Here, I got too much by mistake. You might as well have them.' The quiet man, Derek, thrust a steaming newspaper-wrapped parcel into my hands, turned on his heel and disappeared quickly down the stairs before I had a chance to thank him. I wolfed down the delicious fish and chips, deeply grateful for the first act of kindness I had been shown since I had run away from my family.

I had started to feel a little easier sitting in the residents' lounge and now that Derek Stones was my 'friend' no one gave me any hassle. The men had toned down their ripe language when Derek had told them one night that there was a 'lady' present. 'So mind your fucking mouths,' he said quietly. That word always shocked me and I felt a little uneasy hearing Derek saying it with a scowl to the men seated around the room.

I still didn't go out in the evenings and although a couple of girls at the mill sometimes invited me to join them in the pub I was fearful of being caught. I didn't know what or who would catch me; I just knew that I wasn't allowed to go out at night. Derek had started to walk into my room without knocking. It irritated me when he did this, as he often did now, but I was afraid to tell him, although I wanted to, that I would prefer it if he knocked. I worried that he would be offended and he seemed to be my only friend.

One wet, miserable night, the old television set had broken down and I was sat in my drab room reading when Derek invited me to listen to Radio Luxembourg on his radio in his room with him. I didn't need a second to think about the chance to hear the latest hit parade. I sat on the bed beside Derek in the low-lit room and I was thrilled when he put his arm around my shoulders; it was so romantic being alone with this good-looking man. The dimmed light seemed to loosen Derek's tongue. He told me that he had been abandoned by his mother when he was only three. She had walked out, leaving him and his two brothers alone while his father was serving in Burma during the Second World War.

'Our Eddie were too little to reach the latch on the door.' He ground his teeth as he spoke. 'We was alone for three days in that fucking house, no food, no nothing.' His voice trailed off. I waited for more as he lit another cigarette. 'Any road, the police broke in and we was whipped off to the orphanage in Preston.'

My heart went out to him. At least my real mother didn't walk out while Dad was away. I instinctively hugged him; I knew he was still hurting. Almost without my realising it he was kissing me. Then I didn't know what was happening. Pain shot through me like a hot knife, but I was afraid to cry out in case I annoyed him. Talking about his mother had angered him and it seemed to me that he was taking it out on me. My body felt bruised and almost as bad as when Dad had given me a hiding. But I had never experienced this feeling of feeling dirty and ashamed.

I searched my mind frantically for a way to stop him doing this horrible thing to me. I wanted to be home in my room with the ugly green statue and the painting of the beautiful Welsh valley. I wanted my Daddy to be near by; I knew he would have stopped this awful thing that was happening to me. I wanted to hear my brothers practising how to yodel cowboy songs in the kitchen. I would have even been grateful to hear Jessie's flat monotone voice calling one of the boys to 'stick more coal on't fire'.

But I was lying halfway across Derek's lumpy bed, covered with a dark brown chenille bedspread, paralysed with fear and not able to tell him to stop hurting me because I was afraid I would hurt his feelings. The scent of Palmolive shaving soap mixed with the odour of male sweat assaulted my nostrils. I fixed my gaze on the bare flyblown bulb hanging off-centre from the damp-stained ceiling. Then it was over. The Platters were warbling 'Only yooooou' out of the crackling transistor radio, competing to be heard over the rattling sash windows as he rolled over on to the other side of the bed. He said nothing as he reached for a cigarette. I was deeply shocked and ashamed as I straightened my clothes discreetly and stole out of the dimly lit, mean room back across the landing.

Jessie had said the day she got the letter from Littlewoods Pools telling her that she hadn't after all won the thousands of pounds she thought she had, 'What's for you won't go by you.' That was her way of accepting all the misfortunes that visited her. I had always thought that my future was not in the hands of fate, but in that moment my life changed. Afterwards as I lay awake in my own cold, hard bed, full of fear, tears streaming down my face, wetting the thin pillow where a hundred other heads had lain before me, her words echoed in my mind. Why had I taken that bus from Manchester leaving it to fate where I would end up? I hadn't thought about my future; today was what mattered, my immediate need for shelter and work were uppermost in my mind. I could not have contemplated going back home, I had burned my bridges, but I was utterly unprepared for independent living.

A few weeks before I left Dad had said to me, 'If you ever get into trouble, remember I'm still your father.' I was mystified by what he meant, and maybe he should have explained to me what he meant by 'trouble'; now I knew.

I rolled what had happened around my mind. I knew nothing about sex or what was involved between men and women. I had never given a second thought as to how women got pregnant. I don't even recall hearing the word 'pregnant' and since we had left Ireland I didn't know anyone who had given birth. At school when I heard that one of the girls in my class had allowed a lad to touch her bare breasts I had been revolted and couldn't bring myself to speak to her again. Now I was worse than she was; I was a hussy, and the full meaning of sex became crystal clear to me.

I stayed in my room for several days, ashamed to face anyone, thinking that they would be able to tell what I had done by just looking at me. Derek tried to coax me out, but I just kept the door locked and pretended I wasn't in. A new dread overcame me. Was I pregnant? I didn't know how I could tell and convinced myself that I was. I felt like dying. What a mess and no one to turn to except Derek.

One day the following week I came home from work and found a strange man sitting in my room. 'Derek said it would be OK.'

Betty told me that, as I had moved in with Derek, she had let my room to someone else. Derek had moved all my bits and pieces into his room that morning. I was furious.

'Just get that man out of my room, now!' I shouted at Betty. She smiled maliciously at me; she didn't like me and was enjoying my predicament. I wanted to slap her.

I was now effectively homeless. By the time Derek had returned to the lodgings I was miserable and frightened. Having no immediate target my anger had dissipated. I sat by the window in Derek's room watching the darkness fall over the grimy town skyline, which took on its own kind of stark beauty. I tried to understand what had happened. Was it my fault? Had I given Derek any reason to believe that there was anything between us? Was it perhaps the way I sat on his bed? But there had been no other place to sit. Maybe I had given him, without realising it, signals that I was interested. I blamed myself. I could not have known at that point that he was more emotionally damaged than I was, and that his child-hood had been more painful than anything I had been through. I had sold my life to this man for a meal of fish and chips, or so it seemed to me then.

I prayed for my period to come and then I would get out of this abysmal place and find Maureen in Manchester.

'Two can live cheaper than one. Besides, you wouldn't last much longer on your own,' Derek reasoned matter-of-factly when I asked him what he thought he had been doing. Of course, he was right when he pointed out that I might be pregnant and wouldn't be able to work; how did I think I was going to manage then? I was unable to answer. I felt intimi-dated and helpless. Naive and inexperienced, I felt that I had no choice but to stay put until I was sure I wasn't pregnant, never imagining that I would have to endure what in my mind I referred to as 'it' again.

Derek was a cold, uncommunicative and mostly silent man. We never went out in the evening together and I would feel empty and angry as I watched him getting ready to go out on Fridays and Saturdays. He must be ashamed to be seen with me, I thought. I knew I wasn't pretty or glamorous so I supposed it was understandable. I would iron his shirt and press his trousers and stay up until he came home to make his supper. As he didn't shout or hit me I put up with the situation. Naturally 'it' occurred again and I became trapped in a vicious spiral of waiting for my periods; the weeks turned into months ...

One Saturday morning I was rushing about, getting my weekly shopping, when a sudden violent downpour sent me flying into the indoor market for shelter.

'Excuse me.' A very tall man was blocking the small side door into the market hall. The man turned and for an instant we stared into each other's eyes, recognising each other instantly.

'Ebbs!' It was my father. I didn't wait; I took flight back out into the rain and sprinted back to the lodging house as fast as I could. When I was safely back in the room I shared with Derek I sank to the floor behind the door and waited and wept. Had he followed me? I could hardly breathe and trembled like a leaf until Derek came home from work.

Recently I discovered from conversations with my brothers that Dad tried to follow me that day but lost me in the Saturday crowds. 'She looked so thin and poor,' he told Jessie when he got back to the market. Jessie had no sympathy; she couldn't have cared less what was happening to me, and carried on with her shopping. But at least he knew that I wasn't too far away. He was angry with her when she refused to speak to Mr Rhodes with a view to finding out if he knew where I might be living. Dad put his pride in his pocket and went to see my ex-employer.

'I'll see what I can find out, Mr Doyle,' he said when Dad explained how worried he was.

EIGHT

Dad had trouble all his life from being impulsive. He had met Jessie the night he had landed in England after being forced to have us all committed to the industrial schools. Bit by bit, over the years, I was able to piece together the events that brought Jessie into our already badly damaged family. He met her in the local pub in Holmfirth in Yorkshire while he was looking for a room and Jessie had looked him up and down. He told me one day, 'What a fecking nerve, she wouldn't have looked out of place in a tinker's caravan herself.' He quickly realised that she was very unhappy in her marriage to David. He desperately needed to find a mother for us and get us out of the schools. The terror he had was that the boys would be transferred to the Christian Brothers. I was only a year away from being locked up with the Sisters of Mercy. Neither possibility bore thinking about. 'There's nothing Christian or merciful about those bastards,' he told Jessie as he tried to persuade her to go back to Dublin with him. He wasn't interested in her looks or how she dressed; all he knew was that she kept a clean home and cooked a decent dinner. Somehow he felt 'safe and secure' when she was about and was sure that he was making the right decision in asking her to be a mother to his children.

From the outset it was obvious that Jessie didn't like me. He supposed that it was understandable given the circumstances, but knew that she went too far sometimes. 'Your granddad was right in a way when he told Jessie to lay off you, but I was having no one telling me how to run my life or interfering with the upbringing of my children,' he told me, with some regret in his voice. Granddad's barb that 'You're a cruel bastard treating the children like little slaves' had wounded him deeply. But, he reasoned, Jessie worked hard in the jam factory and what harm could a little housework do?

When Granddad had stormed out of the house that dreadful night saying that he was going back to Ireland, as usual Dad didn't know how to say sorry. 'Well, let him, he can stew in his own juice,' he muttered to himself after Granddad had gone. Then I heard him shout at Jessie, 'The Da was right, just leave Evelyn alone, do you hear me? If it wasn't for you he would still be here.' He slammed the door so hard that the whole house shook and the noise echoed up the street as he left for his bolt hole, the pub.

At the pub he could relax and enjoy himself playing the piano and joining in with the craic. If Jessie had been more careful of her appearance he would have taken her with him. She always looked a sight in her baggy old trousers and big shapeless jumpers. He wouldn't have told her for the world, but why couldn't she wear a brassiere and stop wearing his old underpants? 'There was nothing feminine about her,' he half whispered to me one day, many years later. It didn't occur to him that these things were expensive; the women who went to the pub were always smart and smelled nice, but they weren't trying to keep six kids fed and pay nearly all the bills out of their meagre wages. I am sure that Dad would never have dreamed of going with another woman, even though a good few had tried to hook him – he was above all else loyal and honest; besides, one at a time was enough for him, although Jessie didn't believe him. I am sure that Dad had forgotten how to love. He didn't appear to love Jessie or anyone any more. In his mind loving people only caused pain and, with his mother and sister dying when he was a child and his wife leaving him, he had coped with all the pain he could stand. He could no longer show emotion and he felt empty and tense most of the time.

Dad was worried that growing up in this country, where the kids appeared to rule the parents, we would lose respect for our 'elders and betters'. As far as he was concerned children had a place and that was where his children would stay as long as they were under his roof. Dad sometimes thought that he was perhaps a little hard on us, but firm discipline wouldn't do us any harm. He was appalled that Granddad thought he was cruel. He knew deep down in his heart that sooner or later the whole lot of us would leave him anyway and he would spend his old age alone; hadn't everyone else left him one way or another? It didn't occur to him that he was the one driving everyone away with his uncontrollable temper and sudden mood swings. As young ones we couldn't possibly understand this and lived in constant terror of the next bad temper.

Dad had thought that maybe things would be different if he took his family out of the colourless city where it always seemed to be raining – not the soft rain of home, but hard bone-chilling rain – and where there was nothing green to take the harsh edges off the landscape. That was why he had decided to get away from Manchester. We'll find a place in the country, nearer to your family,' he had told Jessie when she had yet again threatened to leave. He had got used to her being there and knew she would have a hard time starting over again; it was impossible for her to go back to Holmfirth and he felt responsible.

He resolved to try and ease up a bit on the discipline but a sadness hung over him, once Granddad had gone; harsh words could not be unsaid.

It's hard to know how different my life would have been if I had known that Dad was desperate to find me and wouldn't have forced me to go home. Had I known that he would have stood by me whether I was pregnant or not, I would certainly have kept in touch with him. I didn't know that despite the hidings and all the bawling at us he still loved his children and wanted to protect us from the harsh outside world. I found it difficult to believe, though, that Dad had spent endless sleepless nights worrying about my safety and well-being.

The big motorcar seemed to fill the small narrow street and the neighbours hung out of their windows gaping at the unusual sight of two well-dressed businessmen knocking on the filthy door of the lodging house. Betty scraped back her greasy hair with her fingers and looped it through an elastic band in an effort to look tidy, as she hobbled down the dingy hallway to answer the door.

'Wait there, I'll see if she's in,' she told Mr Rhodes, and rudely shut the door in his face as she went up to find me, relieved that they weren't looking for her.

In the few seconds it took for the men to ascend the stairs I managed to kick Derek's shoes under the bed and scoop his toiletries into a drawer.

'Evelyn, your father is worried about you. Will you telephone him?' Mr Rhodes was kind and didn't betray his disgust at my living conditions. He promised that he wouldn't tell Dad my address. He asked me if I was happy and told me that if he could do anything to help me all I had to do was get in touch.

'I'm very happy,' I lied. 'My boyfriend and I are saving up for a deposit on a house. Yes, I'm very happy.' I hoped I sounded convincing. More than anything in the world I would have loved to have got into his big clean car and leave this nightmare I found myself in, but I had my pride and I was feeling very foolish and ashamed to have been found in these circumstances. I agreed to let him give Noel the telephone number of the payphone in the hall; I hoped that my brothers would at least call.

NINE

The sixties were swinging. Beehives and six-inch stiletto heels gave way to mini skirts and cute, knee-length white plastic boots with kitten heels. Nylon tights were cheap enough for ordinary working girls and liberated women from suspender belts, which constantly snapped in the most embarrassing circumstances. Women's lib was all the rage and bras were being burned ceremoniously, mostly by stick-insect thin women – the more well endowed of us clung on doggedly to our Playtex pointed cotton efforts. The Rolling Stones weren't getting satisfaction and the Beatles were having a hard day's night. Boys were letting their hair grow in shaggy manes, wearing flowery patterned clothes and proclaiming 'peace, man' with a casual shrug of the shoulders in a mid-Atlantic accent. Everyone wanted to 'ban the bomb'. Love was free.

An old man at work commented bitterly, 'Bloody poofters, the lot o' them, what they need is another bloody war; aye, that would sort the buggers out.' 'Teenager' was a new word on the lips of newsreaders; they were now the new economic power, being voracious consumers, and there were even shops especially for them. They were all 'with it' and 'cool'.

The Americans and Russians were racing to the moon, but had plunged the world into terror of nuclear war with the stand-off over Cuba. We held our breath as the Russians sailed west across the Atlantic Ocean, wondering if they would turn back in time. President Kennedy was shockingly shot dead in Dallas and we all mourned; Jack Ruby shot dead the alleged assassin Lee Harvey Oswald on a live news broadcast in America. Hippies abandoned free love and became peace demonstrators; they rioted in London protesting about the Americans waging war in Vietnam, fighting policemen and injuring police horses; the country was outraged. The older generation called for the reintroduction of conscription to the army, which had only just been abolished. The Mini motorcar rolled off the production lines at Longbridge and the unions discovered that they had the power to bring the country to its knees. Political parties played musical chairs in and out of Downing Street.

None of this made any difference to me. The 'Swinging Sixties' completely passed me by. I was neither with it nor cool. Days, weeks and months merged seamlessly and monotonously in unbroken drudgery in a variety of low-paid, menial jobs. I had left the cotton mill; the dirt and noise made me ill and breathless. Dr Duddy, wreathed in a blue cloud of cigarette smoke, told me to find different employment. He scribbled out a prescription for antibiotics and suggested that I change the Woodbines for 'something a little less strong'. I started smoking the new tipped cigarettes.

My brothers had been in touch with me for several months now and I lived for their infrequent calls, although each call brought terror that Dad might be on the other end of the line. My brothers assured me that he wasn't aware of our contact.

Derek had said that two could live as cheaply as one but somehow it didn't work out that way. I didn't have a clue where the money went and I was afraid to question Derek about it; we were constantly broke.

'I hear they pay good money on the buses,' I told him one evening when he told me to borrow a couple of pounds from an Irishman who had moved into the lodgings some weeks before. I found the idea of borrowing money every bit as repugnant and shameful as asking for 'tick' at the local corner shop, but I did it. Derek, now driving long-distance lorries, didn't want me to work on the buses, but admitted that we needed the money and agreed that I should apply.

I was very happy working as a bus conductress and often worked double shifts because apart from the extra money, once again I found myself in the situation where my work was my entire social life. No one guessed how miserable I was; I was nicknamed 'laughing girl'. Some of the older ones muttered darkly about young ones being 'money grabbing bastards'. I found myself attracted to a couple of the younger drivers, but when one of them asked me to go dancing with him I refused and feigned outrage. 'I'm a respectable married woman,' I told him. I was ashamed of living 'over t' brush', as they said in Oldham.

One day a familiar figure caught my eye and stopped me dead in my tracks. As I ran towards the warmth and chatter of the staff canteen I saw her sitting on a wooden bench in the cold dirty waiting room of the depot. It was Jessie. I approached her slowly with some trepidation. She saw me but her expression revealed nothing. I didn't expect her to smile at me but I could tell that something was wrong. Had someone had an accident? Was someone dead? I sat down on the bench beside her and was a little surprised to find myself hoping that none of my workmates would see me talking to her; she was dirty looking and shabby. I also felt pity for her. She had an air of desolation, loneliness and neglect about her. I knew she wasn't all bad and I wanted to hug her, but that invisible brick wall was still there; she stiffened when I brushed her with my knee.

'How did you know where to find me?' I asked her, knowing that if she knew where I was Dad would as well. She told me that her friend had seen me. Elsie was Jessie's only 'friend': a friend in the sense that they saw each other only at the mill – she had no social life of any kind. To my horror as I waited for her to tell me why she had sought me out, I realised that I was falling into the same trap that she was in.

'I 'ad t' warn you, lass,' she began, in the maddening slow dull tone of voice that I hated so much. I wanted to tell her to spit it out, but held my tongue as she slowly rolled a cigarette and searched her cavernous red leather shopping bag for a match to light it. At last she levelled her gaze on me. 'Your father is going to apply to the courts to have you deported back to Ireland.' She delicately pinched a stray strand of tobacco off the tip of her tongue with her thumb and middle finger and studied it for a few seconds before discarding it. 'He knows you're living with a lad.'

She got up off the bench and faced me. I felt the blood draining from my face. Not being sure if my legs would hold me, I remained seated.

'That's all I came for.' She turned on her heel.

As I watched her leave with that strange swinging gait of hers, her words echoed in my head. If Dad was to have me deported it would mean only one thing: that he was going to have me committed to a Magdalene laundry. The fact that I was living 'in sin' was more than enough for him to prove that I was immoral and to take me before a court in Ireland; the worst nightmare of my childhood was now a very near reality.

That evening Derek found me throwing my few possessions into an old shopping bag.

'I'm leaving,' I told him as I dashed from place to place, scooping things that belonged to me into the bag. He gripped my wrists and made me stand still while I told him what Jessie had said.

'You're not going anywhere. I'm phoning your father.' He picked up my handbag and started rummaging through it looking for my little notebook. I saw red; how dare he go into my bag I thought. That was my very personal and private property; even Dad had asked me to turn my bag out for him one day when he was searching me for cigarettes. I thought of Jessie and how much I didn't want to be like her, so beaten and weighed down, having been bullied by one person after another throughout her life. Her only retaliation was to hurt and bully those weaker than her. Now at nearly fifty years of age she was a bitter and very unhappy woman. Having been out in the world among 'normal' people for a couple of years I had come to the conclusion that Dad treated Jessie more like a servant than a partner. He had had no role model to learn from as his mother had been ill for a long time during his childhood and so my father had run wild; he had never seen a real family living a normal life. He had not thought of the implications of asking a comparative stranger to be part of his family. I had also noticed that after they had rowed or Jessie had disappeared for a while that things were a little easier.

I tried to snatch my bag back from Derek. 'I don't care what you say or do, I'm going,' I shouted at him.

Before I knew what was happening he slapped me hard across my face. Too shocked to retaliate, I crumpled in a sobbing heap on to the floor.

'You've kidnapped my daughter, you dirty bastard,' my father roared down the phone.

Derek thought he was insane and tried to calm him. 'She's safe with me; it's you she's scared of, you mad bugger!'

It was no use; there was no talking to Dad while he was in this frame of mind and he hung up.

Derek was not about to let me run away from him, and he regretted lashing out at me. He cried as he begged me not to leave him and to forgive him. He didn't know what had come over him. 'I really love you, and I don't want to lose you,' he told me and I believed him. When he said he would rather cut off his hands than hurt me, I believed him.

Secure in the knowledge that I was loved and would be protected by 'my man', I made the decision to go and see my father. I wore my blue jeans and put my hair in a ponytail. In my mind I was going to assert my independence of Dad and I was well aware that wearing jeans would test his acceptance of me as an adult.

TEN

My legs trembled as I walked towards the house. I was regretting my decision to wear the jeans and quickly removed the elastic band holding the ponytail. Dad's shiny blue Hillman was parked on the street. I hesitated before I knocked gently; I still had time to change my mind.

'You, answer the fecking door,' I heard my father shout, as though to an idiot servant. He hadn't changed, but I couldn't have run away if I had wanted to; I was rooted to the bleached scrubbed step.

There is something indefinable about a house where there is no love. A greyness pervades it; nothing shines, least of all the inhabitants, and a heavy silence hangs expectantly, waiting to be broken; the apparent calm is quite deceptive.

Jessie's tea-stained pint mug was on the hearth stone beside a tarnished brass ashtray, and in the grate a mean fire glowed but was failing miserably to radiate any heat. A few brass ornaments carelessly sat on top of the small tiled fireplace. The skimpy old red-and-cream-striped curtains hung limply and neglected from a wire stretched between two large screws over the window.

When I entered the room Dad jumped up from his chair.

'What's up?' His immediate reaction was that I was in trouble and he had a look of fear on his face.

I told him that I was here to discuss his intention to send me back to Ireland.

'Where did you get that stupid bloody idea?' He really

didn't know what I was talking about. He was genuinely shocked when I told him about Jessie's visit to the bus depot.

Boldly I lit a cigarette. 'I'm not going anywhere. I'm engaged to Derek,' I lied, 'and that's that.'

Dad told Dermot to make me a cup of tea and he scurried away. I felt enormous pity for this small boy and wished with all my heart that I could take him away with me, but I held my tongue. I couldn't help any of my brothers just yet and I might make things worse if I said anything.

'Will you not come back?' Dad asked me. He seemed not to notice that I was smoking, or if he did he said nothing. 'Things would be different,' he assured me. We talked as equals and drank our tea. My mind turned over the possibility of moving back home – until Jessie came in.

'What's she doing 'ere?' she demanded, her loathing of me tangible.

I stood up to leave but Dad told me to sit down again, telling her that who was in his house was none of her business. Almost before I knew it I was in the middle of and the subject of a ferocious row. I slipped out unnoticed. Jessie left Dad the next day.

Now I was no longer *persona non grata* and the three older boys felt they could visit me at will. This made my life happier. The boys liked Derek; he was a 'man's man' and of course because my brothers had a friend in him I did anything to keep him happy. But I was still essentially miserable and felt trapped.

Dad asked me to go home whenever I called to see him, and when no amount of coaxing or emotional blackmail worked he turned on me one day. 'And don't come into this house wearing trousers again, you bloody hussy,' he roared. As I slammed out I told him not to worry, I wouldn't come at all. I decided that the only way to get Dad off my back about going home and being the 'dutiful daughter' and taking care of 'your poor oul' Da' was to find Jessie and persuade her to go back. I didn't think I was being selfish at the time, but undeniably I was thinking of myself. Although I was far from happy with Derek, I knew that if I went back home I would end up like so many Irish only daughters: a virtual slave to the male members of the family until they got married and the parents died; and Dad was so big and strong he could live another forty or fifty years. I shuddered at the thought of listening to him shouting about his sausages being burned or the state of his boiled eggs for years more to come. I chose the lesser of two evils and decided that Derek was my best chance. I would never get another chance to meet a nice young man and fall in love like most other girls my age. Hadn't Derek told me that I was 'soiled goods' and men didn't want second-hand girls? I was stuck where I was. Never mind, I thought, I'll just have to make the best of it.

'You can't stay in this place,' I said to Jessie when at last I found her a few weeks after my row with Dad. She had contacted Maurice and he gave me her address. Poor Jessie: if my lodging house was mean and miserable, the filthy dive she was trying to live in was worse. There were five or six Pakistani youths living in each of the rooms and the smell of sweat and curry mingling was overpowering. Their music, very strange to my ears, was blasting from the windows and could be heard halfway down the street. Jessie was sitting in a back room that measured no more than six by eight feet. Her few clothes and a towel were neatly folded on the floor, the narrow divan bed being her only furniture.

'It's all right and t' lads are good to me.' She didn't look at me.

I had to find the right words to persuade her to get out of this dreadful situation. She was very thin and her skin hung in folds from her matchstick-like arms. Her brown eyes were dull and sunk back in her head; her hair hung limply, lank and greasy.

'Jessie, Dad wants you to go home. Anything's better than this dump.' I sat on the divan beside her and offered her a cig-arette. I didn't want her to see my face in case my expression betrayed the real reason for wanting her to go home. But I did genuinely feel pity for her; I would have felt pity for anyone in this awful place. Jessie had worked hard all her life and here she was living in abject poverty and squalor in a ghetto with nothing to show for her life's efforts but a few second-hand clothes and a thin towel. It started to dawn on me that we, my brothers and I, were the probable cause of her relationship with Dad breaking down.

When she and Dad had visited me in the convent I had been jealous of the way they held hands and shared secret little jokes together. When we first came home Dad would kiss her on the lips when he left for work and they always had plenty to talk about. But not long after we moved to Manchester that all changed. Money was tight and the rows started. I supposed that I would have been resentful of a bunch of kids who chained me to grinding hard work and poverty. This wasn't going to happen with Derek and me; I was going to try and love him. Yes, I would even pretend to like 'it', but I was going to get a career and make sure that I didn't have to depend on anyone else for food and shelter. I grew up in the instant I realised that only a very few lucky people had it all and I was not one of them. I would make the best of the situation and even if I had to fight every step of the way to any success I was determined to have it.

Jessie fixed her gaze on a spot just behind my left shoulder and as if to herself she said, almost in a whisper, 'I've deserved it all. I shouldn't have done it, but I would have been dead otherwise.' There was a long heavy silence as I held my breath waiting for more. Finally she shook her head and sighed deeply. An expression of complete surrender and resignation came over her face; but she wouldn't be drawn further.

'Come on, you're getting out of here today.' I took charge and Jessie offered no resistance.

Within the hour I had delivered her back home to Dad. He was appalled at her appearance and immediately had the boys running around making tea, building up the fire and drawing a hot bath for her. My brothers seemed to breathe a collective sigh of relief that Jessie was back. All attention was on Jessie; even the dog seemed to be barking with relief. I left them to it, slipped out of the house unnoticed and ran for a bus back to Oldham. Today would be the first day of the rest of my life.

ELEVEN

I did not bother to go and see Dad and Jessie for more than two years; he picked a fight with me no matter how I tried to avoid one, so I thought it best to leave him alone. I decided to try and find my real mother. Derek understood this, having been brought up in an orphanage and having endured extreme cruelty at the hands of the house 'mother and father'.

When Derek's mother walked out of his life Derek and his older brother Eddie had huddled together under a dirty thin blue blanket in the cold dark room; the baby was still in the big pram where their mother had left him. They had no idea how long it had been since their mother had said she was going out, but Eddie knew that it had been a very long time, and they were very frightened.

Derek remembered his mother saying 'Your father's buggered off t' war and I'm getting out of this 'ole' before she left. He didn't remember ever having a dad; not many of his little pals in the street had dads, although some of them said that they had them.

Eddie and Derek didn't like 't' rent man' who came and banged on the door. They would be told to be quiet and pretend they were not there, and they would all duck down behind the sofa until their mother said it was all right to come out. 'But sometimes she let him in and she would take him upstairs to her bedroom.' Derek and I would be lying in the dark late at night when he talked to me of the horrors of his childhood, and often he would talk until the small hours. When he told me this, he put his hands to his ears involuntarily. 'We could hear her crying out, and the light in the ceiling would shake.' When 't' rent man' had gone their mother would be in a terrible temper and sometimes she would slap the boys and shout at the baby to stop 'that bloody bawling'. 'Eddie and me would try to make her smile, but Mam hadn't smiled in a long time.'

But when she left they wished that she would just come home; they were hungry and cold and the baby smelled awful.

Eddie had dragged a kitchen chair to the wall and snapped on the brown light switch but nothing happened; he continued snapping the switch for a minute or two, but still the room remained dark. Derek didn't like the dark and he was very frightened, but glad that the baby had stopped screaming; there was just the occasional whimper from the pram. Derek laid on an old coat that was hanging from a nail on the back door over the baby. The radio had stopped playing ages ago. 'The bloody sixpence had run out in the meter.' The milk had tasted funny and had little bits floating on the top, but it was all they could find in the kitchen.

Eddie told Derek to mind the baby, as he was going to try and find their mother. Derek became terrified when he saw Eddie crying. 'She had locked the fucking door behind her and our kid couldn't get out.' Anger filled his voice and he swore again, remarking bitterly what a 'cow' his mother was. 'We yelled our heads off, but no one came, and then it got dark,' he continued. I wept silently, knowing the despair of those tiny children, and I felt a rage against Derek's mother that I never felt against my own.

'The next thing I know is the window was being smashed from outside.' Derek had no idea how long they had been on their own. The boys were too tired to get up from the couch.

'Someone was shouting outside for the police to be called, and old Mr Ellis from next door climbed through the window.'

I didn't want to hear any more that minute, but he was in full flow and I felt that he needed to talk; he needed to heal the mental scars. I at least had my brothers and I had been able to spend many hours licking the wounds clean, as it were, by talking and laughing with them about the horrors of our childhood. Derek had not spoken to anyone before about this dark time and I was a willing listener, not least because he was generally a silent partner. Somehow I felt privileged to be his confidante. I urged him to go on.

'Suddenly the tiny room was filled with people. Big strong men in uniforms wrapped us in white soft blankets edged with red lettering, lifted us and, talking soothingly, carried us out and put us in an ambulance.' "CHILDREN ABANDONED BY CALLOUS MOTHER" the headline in the local evening paper screamed. A police spokesman said that the boys aged between about eighteen months and five years had been in the house on their own for three days at least. Their inquiries were continuing in the search for the mother. 'They said that they assumed my father was abroad fighting for his country. The police applied for a place of safety order and we were dumped in bloody orphanages.'

Mrs Robertson didn't like Derek very much, even though he tried his best to please her. She and Mr Robertson were the 'house mother and father' in the Kirkham Cottage Homes in Preston. Derek half remembered that he had a couple of brothers somewhere but he couldn't be sure. He knew that he definitely had a mother and he often wished she would come back and take him home. So many of the boys in the home had no mam or dad – they had 'copped it' in something called the war, and they were going to get the Gerri's, whatever they were, when they grew up. He wondered if he would be able to get Gerri's. 'I didn't know what "copped it" was and I secretly hoped that my dad had copped it; it sounded to me like a nice thing to have happen to you.' He laughed at the childish memory.

One day as he washed the four wide steps at the front of his home cottage he became aware that a bigger boy from the other end of the complex was standing watching him. He kept his eyes averted. Derek had learned that eye contact could bring trouble pouring down on his head.

'Hey kid.' He looked up from the bucket of dirty water and saw that the boy looked somehow familiar.

'Are you our Derek?' the boy asked.

Derek said nothing. He stood up to face the bigger boy, nervously twisting the wet rag in his hands.

Eddie, at nearly eleven, had grown into a strapping lad over the five years he had been in the vast complex of the homes. Each age group was separated into groups of twenty in each cottage. Only now as Eddie passed the age of ten did he have the freedom to move about the complex and look for his little brothers. He was enraged when he saw Derek looking like a slave washing concrete steps in the bitter cold of November. He yanked the sleeve of the younger boy's jersey and half dragged him the quarter mile or so back to his own home cottage to face the house father.

'He's not going back there and that's final,' he said. 'We'll run away if you make him.'

Mr Barry looked at the earnest face set like an old man and the miserable little scrap he had dragged through the door. 'Now then lad, 'tis me what gives t' orders round 'ere.'

Derek was taken into the Barrys' home cottage. He found out later that he and other members of staff had suspected the Robertsons of cruelty towards their charges and had voiced their concerns to the local authority, but there was a war on and staff were hard to come by. However, if they had proof, the authorities would have to act; but that was for later. Now he had to deal with a very tricky situation.

'One day we were told that we had a visitor, our first since we had been put there. This small thin man was telling us that he was our dad. "Me and t' missus are bringing you all 'ome," he told us. I was scared; home was a distant memory and I remembered only the bad things that happened at home.'

It was 1952, ten years since their mother had abandoned her little boys. She was never found. When Eddie senior was demobbed from the army in 1947 he was shocked to discover that no one knew where his family were. It had taken him a year to find out that his boys were in an orphanage in Preston. He decided that they were best left where they were until he could get back on his feet. That was more difficult than he had anticipated, as four years in the Burmese jungle had left him weak and ill. A couple of years after his demob he had met Maggie, a widow, and as she had a young son they decided that his boys would have to stay where they were for the time being. He hadn't been to visit them. 'It'll just upset them,' he reasoned, excusing himself.

When Eddie suggested that it was time Maggie's lad thought about getting out and earning 'a bit o' brass' this didn't go down too well with her. 'Not bloody likely. He's 'aving an edication whether you bloody like it or not,' she threw at him. She suggested that it was time he took his lads out of the homes. 'Your lads are ready for t' mill now if you need extra brass.'

And so they decided to bring the boys home to Saddleworth. Young Eddie, as he came to be known, was apprehensive. He suspected, rightly, that his father's motive for taking a sudden interest in having his boys home was to send them out to work, but he would go along with it until it suited him otherwise. The boys had learned the hard way that you had to look out for number one, and for your brothers of course.

'I would follow Eddie whatever he said,' Derek told me. 'I had no opinion about anything but knew that as long as I stuck with Eddie I would be all right. Hadn't he looked out for me all this time? And hadn't he rescued me from the nightmare that was the Robertsons' home cottage?' When Jamie, the youngest, had joined them in the Barrys' home cottage a couple of years later, they had both looked out for him together.

The boys heard the ferocious row that followed and a couple of weeks later Jamie was sent back to the home. He had apparently been accused of gouging his name into the new furniture; he was obviously going to be a delinquent.

At Derek's father's house Maggie was the undisputed boss and her son came first, second and last as far as she was concerned. Her husband's older son started at the local transport company as a driver's mate and soon Derek was at the mill. Maggie reckoned that these two extra wage packets would be enough to see her son through the further 'edication' he needed to ensure that his future would be without struggle. The youngest son got on her nerves. 'I can't cope with the young 'un,' she told her husband and broached the subject of sending him back to the home until he was a bit older. 'It'll only be for a couple of years, and we can have 'im 'ome at t' weekends,' she cajoled.

'I 'ad no choice, son,' Eddie and Derek were told by their father. Eddie called him a cowardly bastard and packed his bags and moved into his boss's house further out of the village. 'He told us that he thought it was for the best that Jamie was sent back to the home,' Derek said to me bitterly. A year later his father cried when he informed Derek that Jamie had been adopted by a couple down in Birmingham. 'I lashed out at the old man, knocking him to the floor.'

From then on Derek became silent, morose and completely self-contained; in future he would rely on no one and he resolved to get out of his father's life as soon as he was able to support himself. Jamie was never heard of again.

The day Derek turned seventeen he joined the army and was unlucky enough to be just in time to be sent to Malaya, where a raging 'emergency' was being waged against the native people who wanted their country back from the British after nearly two hundred years watching them getting rich on its resources.

Derek was badly wounded: a long machete opened a ten-inch gash down his chest. 'The commies used to leave little kiddies in the jungle near our camp knowing we wouldn't just leave them there, and they would run off in the night and lead the buggers to us.' He fingered the long white scar that cut though his hairy muscular chest. He didn't seem angry at the Malay native who had nearly taken his life. 'It was war,' he said simply and shrugged.

He left the army and the army took no further interest in him. 'I did six years just to show the old man that I could. He used to say that I wasn't man enough.'

Derek had been engaged to the daughter of his company sergeant major, but he caught her with another soldier. 'Slags, the bloody lot of them,' he said, almost to himself.

I lay awake long after he had finally gone to sleep. I would try never to hurt him, I resolved.

When Angela, my friend from my childhood in Fatima Mansions, sent Granny's death notice to me, futile anger and frustration filled me. I had just been to Ireland, returning home only a couple of days ago, and Granny had died on the very day I had landed in Ireland. I had called at her house in Dùn Laoghaire in the hope of finding the other half of our family, my real mother included. Granddad had left us and we were in touch with no other relatives we could call our own, which caused a certain loneliness, an isolation that cannot be readily explained to others. Hasn't everyone got cousins, aunts and uncles, grandmas and granddads? My brothers and I were the only family we each had.

I found Angela's mother, Mrs Sullivan, though.

'What the feck do you want?' When I introduced myself her voice was harsh and her face unfriendly.

I was shocked and upset. 'Don't you remember me?' Tears were close to the surface, but I held them at bay as I explained that I was Dessie Doyle's daughter.

Suddenly I was enveloped in a massive bear hug as she laughed. 'What the feck are you standing on the doorstep for? Get in out of there.' She almost dragged me into her home.

Nothing had changed much; the house was still full of what seemed to me dozens of children. She explained that because I had an English accent she thought I was an ex-daughter-in-law who had run off and left one of her sons in the lurch. 'The bitch from hell,' she called her and I was glad I was not that Evelyn.

I enjoyed and savoured Mrs Sullivan's home for a brief few days. She insisted I stayed, although space was at a premium, and I shared a large bed with Angela and her two sisters, where we talked girl talk and giggled well into the night. Very reluctantly I said my goodbyes. I felt a void forming; what I had missed by not having a 'normal' life. I had seen a poor but very happy household in action and at close quarters. There had been no anger in the small irritations that cropped up from time to time. I was aware of a total lack of tension, and although my presence must have added some strain to the already cramped conditions there were no undercurrents of resentment from anyone. Mrs Sullivan had fitted me seamlessly into her large brood and within a couple of hours was treating me like a daughter. When she said, 'Here you! Set the table,' I didn't take offence or feel that if I didn't do it properly there would be a row; that was the way families got on with the daily business of life and it wasn't necessary to walk on eggshells for fear of giving offence.

I realised then that being poor wasn't a bar to being happy. As the boat steamed back towards Liverpool I felt a huge sadness and a certain anger at both my parents for depriving my brothers and me of a happy childhood.

The tiny scrap from the *Irish Independent* was my best lead yet in my search for my real mother. I wrote to the address in the death notice and enclosed a sealed letter for my real mother asking for it to be passed on if possible. I didn't hold out much hope. None of her side of the family, apart from Granny, had been in contact with us since the day she had walked out. How could they know anything about us or our whereabouts? Dad had decided to shear off my mother's side of the family.

TWELVE

Oh! How many torments lie in the small circle of a wedding ring!

I don't know why the quotation came to mind; it was as though Granddad was beside me.

My wedding day dawned dark and ominous. I knew I was making a huge mistake. But it was I who had insisted we got married. The shame of living 'over t' brush' was more than I was prepared to stand for. Our relationship had improved in some ways. Since the day I had taken Jessie home I had demanded a more equal share of the relationship and very soon discovered, as most women do early on in the same situation, that withholding 'it' got me exactly what I wanted. I wanted friends and nights out occasionally. I also wanted a career. I started training to be a psychiatric nurse, even though my salary was literally half what I earned on the buses; it was what I wanted and I went ahead without asking or discussing it with Derek.

Now I sat in the taxi next to Derek with my entire wedding party – my brother John and his pal Chris – on the way to the register office and wept. John asked me if I wanted to change my mind. 'It's not too late you know,' he told me kindly and patted my arm. Derek didn't care one way or the other whether we were married or not and told me not to be a 'silly cow'. Of course I wanted to change my mind.

I had harboured silly romantic ideas of what my ideal wedding day would be like: Dad leading me down the aisle to a handsome young man with whom I was madly in love. I would be wearing a beautiful white gown with yards of train and all my brothers would be there, looking on proudly; my real mother would be weeping quietly into her lace handker-chief. But here I was in an old taxi, wearing a coat I had gone to work in with crêpe-paper carnations John had brought to make the occasion a little more special.

The ceremony itself was swift and perfunctory. There were three other wedding parties in the waiting room to come after us. The tears flooded down my face as the lady registrar asked: 'Do you take this man, Derek Stones, to be your lawful hus-band?' I was barely able to answer and her brisk business-like voice changed to one of concern when she asked, 'Are you all right, my dear? No one's forcing you to do this, are they?'

I shook my head in reply and almost before I knew it I was a married woman. I kept my head down as we walked through the other waiting parties and out on to the street.

A few days later, when I got the few photographs that we had taken at the back of the register office, at my brother's insistence, I was horrified to see that I had stood under a sign on the wall behind me that said 'PUBLIC LAVATORIES' and a little hand with the index finger pointing to a place past my left shoulder. I burned them.

What was it that brought terror when the telegram boy knocked on the door? After all, my generation grew up after the war and had no real reason to fear bad news. But my heart was in my mouth as I signed shakily for the little brown enve-lope. I searched my bag and found a sixpence for the boy, impatient for him to be gone.

'Phone the number below after 6 p.m. News of your mother,' it said. I had four hours to wait.

Minnie Lally, an old tramp lady whom I had befriended a

few months before, called. I told her excitedly that I had found my real mother after all these years and she was desperate to see me. A slight exaggeration, of course, as I had no idea if that was so – or indeed who had sent the telegram. Minnie listened gravely as I prattled on. As I gathered up the cups, hoping Minnie would take the hint to go, she said, 'Don't expect too much, lass. Just don't expect it to be all roses.'

I dismissed her comments. How could she possibly know what it was like to find your mother, having been without her for most of your life? Poor Minnie had no one at all in the world. She didn't want anyone and, naive as I was, I knew that she only used me for occasional shelter and a few bob now and then for a packet of cigarettes. I didn't mind; I was happy to be there for her when she needed me. Sometimes I didn't see her for months and I would wonder if she had died; then she would turn up from nowhere and pick up where she had left off.

The voice was instantly recognisable.

'Is that you, Mammy?' I had no trouble whatsoever saying 'Mammy'. The years seemed to roll away; my real mother was on the other end of the line and I was seven again. Our conversation was brief. I found it upsetting that she wasn't actually with me. All the years of longing for my real mammy were finally over. All I could do was cry with relief, healing tears that soothed my soul and lifted my heart; now I would be whole again.

We arranged to meet, and the next few weeks before we were to be reunited crawled by. I rearranged my holidays so that I could visit her. Thoughts of her filled my mind. I imagined conversations we would have. I had decided, even before I had received the telegram, that maybe she'd had good reason for walking out on Dad all those years ago. I remembered the rows and screaming in our home during my early childhood, but all the neighbours in the flats seemed to fight and row with their husbands; weren't we just normal like everyone else? But I did remember always taking Daddy's side. I thought back with warmth to the happy times when I would walk down Cork Street with my mother to the Vincent De Paul canteen and make a show of her by refusing to eat yet again the black pudding that always seemed to be on the menu; to the times when she had a few coppers to spare and we would call into a cake shop on the way home for a Vienna loaf and currant slices, liberally covered with icing sugar. I can still smell the salty sea air that hit us when we would get off the tram when we went to visit Granny. The smell of lavender polish filled her beautiful home and even today the smell of fresh apples brings her large, bright kitchen instantly to my mind. Such times were few and far between and I treasured them.

I don't really know what I expected from my real mother when I travelled to Scotland to meet her for the first time. When she introduced me to her other four children as 'someone I used to look after when her mammy was in hospital' I held my tongue. But I felt shocked and hurt: why was she denying me as her daughter? She later told me that she hadn't had time to tell them about me and my brothers, and she hadn't come looking for us because she was afraid to meet Dad. She was sympathetic, in a detached sort of way, when I told her of our home life since we had been taken out of the schools. Surprisingly, she didn't even ask if it had been hard in the industrial school or if I had been lonely without my brothers. It was with a sinking heart that I realised that it might have been a mistake to find her. The fantasy mother I had built up in my mind was quite different to this reality. I decided, when Derek and I discussed it, that perhaps more time was needed to re-establish the bond that had been broken when she had walked out on us.

Derek and I moved to Glasgow to be near my new-found family, and soon my brothers joined us one by one, Kevin and Dermot moving in with my mother, until only Maurice was left at home with Dad and Jessie. Dad blamed me for decimating his family. It didn't occur to him that the boys found it impossible to stay in a home where light and laughter were rare commodities.

I soon realised that my mother was the undisputed boss of her household. Within a short space of time, it became apparent to me that my mother didn't consider my brothers and me to be her family; we were in the past and it seemed she would have left us there given the choice. However, Kevin and Dermot were working and contributing a significant part of their wages to her household. Dermot later told me that out of his wages of seven pounds she took six and told him, 'You have to give some to Mammy.' Conditioned to obeying without question, he handed over his pay packet.

I began to dislike my mother intensely, although I was growing fond of my half-brothers and -sisters. Derek got on well with them. I think he thought that at last he was part of a real family. I found it easy to like Gerry, my father's cousin and the man my mother had left with, and felt completely at ease in his company. Although he was the spitting image of my father, but not as tall, he exuded a very different persona. He was calm and gentle, spoke in soft measured tones and laughed a lot. His father, my great-uncle Stephen, was a lovely old gentleman, who moved around the house like an apologetic ghost and seemed to be afraid of everyone. He was treated like a household servant by my mother. She referred to and called him 'Mr Talbot' with great contempt, and he stayed in his room as much as possible. This irritated me, and I frequently invited him to my home for lunch and a bottle of beer. Beer was a treat that was totally forbidden by my mother.

'Are you sure she won't smell it on my breath?' he would

ask nervously as I saw him off on his bus back home to prepare the evening meal for her family.

'Not unless you're planning on kissing her,' I would joke
back.

He would laugh and pull a face, indicating that this would
never happen. I eventually persuaded him to go and live with
his daughter in Manchester.

As the weeks passed, I noticed that Dermot wasn't thriving
as he should have been, given that he was now living in a
'happy family' environment. His quiet but alert behaviour
was in stark contrast to that of the noisy boisterousness of the
other four children in the house. When I questioned him he
assured me that everything was OK. 'You must tell me if
you're unhappy,' I told him whenever I saw him.

My visits to my real mother's house became less frequent.
She didn't really seem to be my 'mammy' any more; she was
wrapped up in her second family and I felt like an intruding
stranger. We didn't do mother and daughter things together,
like shopping on Saturdays or meeting up for coffee. She
didn't talk about her family in Ireland, my aunts, uncles and
cousins, or reminisce about the past. There were constant
anecdotes about her four children, but none of my brothers
and me. It was as if we had not existed at all in her earlier life.
Photographs of her four youngsters littered the walls and cab-
inets of her home, but she had not one picture of any of us. It
was not as though she could not have got any photographs of
us before she left us in Fatima Mansions, as photography was
Dad's hobby and he had literally hundreds from which she
could have chosen.

'I've run away.' Dermot was standing at the door of my tene-
ment flat on the other side of Glasgow from where my mother
lived. It had been six months since he had left Dad and come
to Scotland for a better life. Jessie hated Dermot and had given

him such a hard time when I left home that one day the poor lad had snapped and pushed her roughly against the kitchen wall. Fortunately Dad hadn't believed her and Dermot escaped the beating that he fully expected. Like me, he was almost past caring what happened to him, but when he got the opportunity to escape he grabbed it with both hands. I had persuaded him that everything would be different when he had his own mother to care for him.

Now I was filled with rage that my youngest brother felt such despair that he had run away again. Why did his father have no compassion for his youngest son, institutionalised when he was only a baby? How could Jessie, or any woman for that matter, have an almost pathological hatred for a child so small and helpless, but willing to please at all costs? What was it about this young man that he could be rejected yet again by his mother? No one was going to hurt him again, I decided.

'I never want to see you again,' I told my mother during the heated row we had when I went to collect Dermot's belongings. I left her weeping what I thought were 'crocodile tears'.

The last time I saw my mother was about four or five months later on Christmas Eve in 1967. After that day, I never saw her again.

I didn't grieve for the loss of my mother. I had lost her fourteen years before when I watched her get on a bus and, with the instinct and insight of a child, had known that she was never coming back. Maybe I had put her on too high a pedestal. I probably expected too much from the renewed relationship. At what point had the bond been broken? Was it the day she walked out of Fatima Mansions? Was it the day she left me when she visited me in the convent, despite my pleas to her not to go? Could it have been when she had introduced me as a 'someone' to her new family? I have never been able to discover exactly when I really lost her. I decided that the only thing was to get on with my life and move on. Millions of people get by very well without a mother; I was now one of them.

THIRTEEN

George was a workmate of Derek's in the engineering works in Glasgow. Derek still didn't like taking me out where we might have to interact with other people, but George had persuaded him to take me to the company's annual dance. During the weeks leading up to the night I was so excited: this would be my very first big occasion. I managed to buy a beautiful long pink satin sheath dress for just under £2 at the local market. It hung on a hanger on the back of my bedroom door where I would gaze at it and imagine the wonderful time I was going to have for a brief moment in what had become my very ordinary humdrum life – the sort of life that millions of women up and down the country were leading, juggling work and home chores, trying to make the money stretch until Friday, with an occasional night out to the cinema.

I fell head over heels in love. I recognised it immediately. George asked me to dance. His eyes seemed to bore a hole right though me.

'You're very lovely,' he told me.

I was acutely embarrassed and blushed to my roots but couldn't drag my eyes from his face. I wanted this dance to go on for ever. I knew that when the music stopped I would not, could not, see him again. He wasn't the best-looking man I had ever met, but there was an openness about his face that made him very attractive.

'Are you happy with Derek? Is he good to you?'

I swallowed the hard lump in my throat. I wanted to tell

him that no, I wasn't happy – what was happy anyway? I wanted to tell him that I wanted to be young and alive, as I felt at that minute. How could I tell him that, for two pins, I would have gone out the door with him. I had met him not more than three hours before, but from the moment he shook my hand when Derek introduced us I felt as though I had known him all my life.

'Of course I'm happy,' I again lied for the second time that he put the question to me.

George filled my being. I didn't sleep, but never felt tired. My appetite disappeared, and I thought of him every waking minute of the days that followed. Several times I cried for no apparent reason. Fortunately, Derek did not appear to notice and when he told me that he had invited George over for a meal he was puzzled when I told him that under no circumstances was he to bring George to our flat.

'What did he do to you?' I told him not to be stupid – it was just that I didn't like him. Derek seemed satisfied with that. Of course I wanted to see George, but I didn't trust myself to resist him. I knew he felt the same way about me when I looked in his eyes as we said goodnight after the dance. It was better not to put any temptation in the way. I couldn't bring myself to hurt Derek.

Derek landed a very good job in a distillery on the Hebridean island of Islay. As I watched the ferry steaming out of the Tarbert loch tears streamed down my face. He was going ahead of me until I could join him six weeks later. The parting brought the realisation that I loved him, but in a different way to the all-invasive feelings I had for George.

Derek clung to me and wept as we said goodbye

'You will come over, won't you?' It was almost a plea. He loved me and needed me much more than I needed him. My heart bled for him; I had been harsh and bad-tempered with him for weeks and although leaving him was never a course I had planned, it must have seemed to him that at best I only tolerated him. I locked George away; I would get over him. I did, but it took many years.

'Of course I'll come over,' I told him as I brushed his lapels down with my fingertips and straightened his tie. I kissed him lightly on his cheek and gave him a gentle push in the direction of the ferry. I watched the ferry until it disappeared into the mist on the Sound of Islay.

I had burned my bridges. I loved my career and in particular I enjoyed the sense of achievement it gave me, an uneducated mill hand. But there was no going back now, I realised, as I stood in Matron's office to tell her that I was leaving in four weeks' time.

At first I had thought that the nurses' attitude to patients was cold and business-like. A few weeks into my training I watched as two senior nurses discussed the latest film as they dressed a patient who had died only minutes before. I was appalled at their seeming disrespect for the dead woman. But I quickly realised that in order to do the job properly and to give the best care to all the patients, it is impossible to get too involved.

'It is their relatives who mourn the dead, nurse,' the staff nurse informed me. There were exceptions to the rule, especially in a long-stay hospital such as the psychiatric hospital in which I worked. I became very fond of several old ladies in my ward. A lot of our old ladies had no visitors from one end of the year to the other. I'm not blaming their families too much – they must have thought there was no point when the loving mother they once had no longer even recognised them, or had become foul-mouthed and violent. Some of our patients were not 'ill' in the true sense of the word, but had been committed by husbands many years before when all that was needed to have a wife certified was for a husband to tell the doctor that his wife was 'a screaming lunatic'.

One of my patients in the locked psychiatric ward, Agnes Monroe, had been emotionally blackmailed by her elderly, domineering mother into giving up her dream of getting married to the only man she had ever loved. She had met him late in life, just when she had given up all hope of ever finding love. As the weary years rolled on, her mother became more demanding as she became infirm and bedridden. Agnes cracked one night and brought down an axe on her mother's head, silencing her once and for all. The court found her insane and unfit to plead. She was ordered to be detained in a secure psychiatric hospital. 'Nurse, do you think they would know what I had done if I went Australia?' she would ask a thousand times a day, pacing up and down all the while. To her it wasn't the fact that she had murdered her mother that caused her shame; it was that people knew about it.

Another of our patients was the mother of a big television star of the time, and I ran foul of him.

'I am sorry, sir, you will have to wait until the ladies finish lunch,' I told him when he insisted that I let him in to see his mother, who had been suffering from senile dementia for a considerable length of time.

Drawing himself to his full height of about five foot four he bellowed, 'Do you know who I am?'

Gazing down at him I tried to keep a straight face and told him that I didn't care if he was Jesus Christ himself – he would have to wait until lunch was finished.

Matron tried to be cross but her eyes twinkled as she admonished me, 'Really, Nurse Stones, taking the Lord's name in vain is quite unacceptable.' I bobbed a shallow curtsey and fled from her office; I heard her coughing as I closed the door behind me.

On Mondays I loved the smell of the pretty uniforms of blue dresses and very stiffly starched aprons with the collars we attached by little brass studs and we would 'rustle' as we made our way to the wards. At Christmas most of us would parade through the corridors holding lighted candles with our cloaks turned to the red side and sing carols; my eyes would well up when some of our ladies recognised that it was Christmas. It was desperately hard work for pathetically low salaries, but most of us found it rewarding. Many of us had a quiet corner where we could go and have a little weep in private when a favourite lady died, or when we assisted when patients were subjected to what I considered to be the most barbaric treatment of ECT, or electro-convulsive therapy. Their poor bodies would convulse violently and patients would have a crushing headache for days afterwards; I wish I knew if it worked.

Some of the nurses were as mad as the patients. One older nurse was a diagnosed kleptomaniac and the sister in charge of the nurses' home would retrieve mountains of sheets and pillowcases from her room. We were assured that she would never touch our personal belongings, and she didn't. Another would rush around all through the shift with a pillowcase over her arm; she didn't do anything exactly that any of the rest of us could see, but her entertainment value was without price. One day a very harassed doctor told her to answer his bleeper and to his wide-eyed amazement, and ours, she grabbed his lapel and shouted into it, 'Hello, the doctor is a bit busy now. Call back later.' I hesitate to say that she was Irish, but she was.

Now Matron was wishing me well and she hoped I would continue with what she called a very promising career.

It was late in May 1969 when once more I found myself aboard a ferry steaming me to a new life. I stood on the deck for the two-hour sail across the sound, marvelling at the beauty of the islands that nestled like jewels on the unusually calm sea and breathing the clean, salty air. I left the grimy city with her gloomy, tall tenements silently standing guard, blocking out any sunshine that dared to shine on narrow, grey streets where there was nothing green growing.

The pretty little harbour of Port Askaig came into view. Brightly coloured fishing boats jostled and bobbed in the gentle lapping of the waves as they washed up to the shore. A row of whitewashed cottages huddled at the foot of a rocky cliff that took a winding narrow road up to the rest of the island. A small knot of people watched as the ferry docked, but they were not waiting for anyone in particular: they were just watching the comings and goings of the boats.

I looked over the scene and spotted Derek leaning on an old red Mini; staring into the distance, casually smoking a cigarette. In the six weeks since I had waved him off, I had found it difficult to conjure up his image in my mind. He didn't appear to be waiting for anyone either. There was a stillness, a kind of self-containment about him that forbade intrusion to his privacy. I watched him from my position on the deck as the crew and shore staff brought the large red-and-white ferry to rest. He had lost a little weight and gained a slight tan. I thought how handsome he looked and felt pride that he was waiting for me. Not once did he glance at the docking ferry; he stared resolutely ahead at the Paps of Jura, ignoring the busy goings on around him. Later he told me that he was afraid to look in case I had not come.

A casual observer might have assumed that I was being met by a brother or a workmate. Neither of us rushed to the other.

'You made it, then,' he said casually by way of greeting. As we drove along the one-track, winding road towards the village that was to become my new home, his answers to my many questions were stilted and curt. He was like a stranger who had just happened to be travelling my way and had given me a lift.

I gave up trying to get him to talk for the time being and concentrated on the passing wild landscape. The road meandered though heather-covered peat bogs to the distant shoreline of the north-east end of this island known as the Queen of the Hebrides. Small, whitewashed farmhouses were scattered here and there, relieving the brown monotony of the moors. At last, a sharp bend took us down a steep incline and I saw the village spread out before me.

Bunnahabhain, or as Derek correctly pronounced it 'Bonahavan', was one of eight fine malt distilleries on this tiny island. Most of them had started as illicit stills run by wily crofters to supplement meagre incomes; Bunnahabhain had been in existence for about one hundred years and was now run by a large company based on the mainland.

The few villagers out and about stared into the car; some of them waved to us. I smiled and waved back. Derek said, 'Nosy gits!' He pulled the car up outside a neat house at the end of a terrace not more than thirty yards from the shore, looking out across the Sound of Islay to the mysterious brooding island of Jura. I was going to make this marriage work if it killed me, I promised myself. I felt at home; there was air to breathe and the palette of my world was now the rich browns and purple of the moors and heather, the gold of spectacular sunsets and every shade of grey to blue of the sea and sky, depending on whether Mother Nature was angry or not. There was still nothing green, or not much, but I was happy to be there; it was a pretty place.

It took me a while to 'tune' into the soft, sing-song accents of the islanders where most of the old people spoke Gaelic as their first choice of language, but as their ancestors were Irish I was sure I would fit in fairly quickly. How wrong could I be.

These people considered the inhabitants of the mainland to be from another planet. Of course the island was staunchly Protestant, but not just Protestant: they were Free

Presbyterians, whose faith was based strictly on the Scriptures. Some of the old die-hards kept the Sabbath literally for prayer alone. No one, and I failed to notice this, hung washing on the line on Sunday.

'You're a dirty Irish pig,' a fat, red-faced young woman told me as I swept my doorstep one morning about three months after I had arrived. 'Why don't you go back where you belong?' And she turned on her heel, leaving me totally confused about what I had done to offend her. Although she had put a considerable amount of venom into her words, I smiled as I watched her waddle past the bond warehouse. Her intention to anger me had been futile in that the nasty words sounded musical and lyrical in her soft burr. Old Annie McLean, who lived two doors away told me that although she had lived in the village for more than thirty years, the locals still considered her to be an 'outsider'. 'And you have nay chance, lass.' I was apparently too sophisticated, coming from 'the big city', for their simple ways. 'And they know you must be Catholic because you hang your washing out an Sundays,' she told me with a twinkle in her eye. I liked Annie and Margaret, another 'outsider'. Gradually the younger women in the village appeared to accept me, although I found it amusing that they hardly ever used my Christian name – it was always 'Mrs Stones'; but I was never invited to join village activities except when they had no choice or excuse for not inviting me.

I didn't care about any of this; I was building a happy marriage to Derek. My brothers were regular visitors. I took a job in the cottage hospital and we went to some of the ceilidhs in Bowmore, the main town, where I learned country dances. I thought my life was complete. Although Derek and I had some rough patches, when I regretted my decision to join him on the island, on the whole I was happy enough. That is until a tear-stained letter arrived just over a year later.

'Dear Ebbs ...' it began. I was in two minds whether to read it or put it straight on the fire. Whenever Dad came back into my life it was totally disrupted. He had managed to fall out with all his children one by one and instinct told me that he wanted something; he usually didn't write to enquire about how we were doing. 'I was wondering how you were keeping and thought I would try and get up to see you for a few days,' his letter went on. I knew I should have stopped reading but with a lemming-like irresponsibility I read on. 'It can be for only a few days; Jessie and I want to have a touring holiday in Scotland.' He had underlined 'only' and 'few', so why was I worried? Because a little voice in my head was saying, 'He's after something!'

I polished and scrubbed for days; this would be the first time my father had seen my home. I was determined that he would have nothing to throw back at me in the event of a row. There was sure to be one sooner rather than later.

'Jasus, it's a great place this.' Dad sniffed the bracing air appre-ciatively. He had driven in his little blue van all the way from Devon, where he and Jessie had been living. Jessie had been stuck in the back with their two dogs sitting cramped on an old armchair that Dad had cut the legs off. The van was stuffed to the roof with boxes and a cold feeling gripped my heart when I spotted a teapot and a thick glass vase sticking out of the top of one: nobody took glass vases on holiday. I tried to dismiss from my mind the certain knowledge that he had moved house. 'Oh God! Not to my house,' I prayed silently.

I was not too surprised to find that God hadn't been listen-ing to me. A few days after he arrived Dad said, 'You know Ebbs, I think I would like to settle down here.' He told me that he couldn't bear to go back to Devon now that Maurice had decided to go to Australia with some friends. Dad sobbed when he asked me to speak to Maurice and try to persuade him not to go. I did, and Maurice didn't go, but many years later Maurice told me that he wished he had.

The 'few days' turned into three months and my nerves were shattered. Dad had claimed his 'spot', as it were, in our home. To my amazement, he didn't pick a row with me in all that time; in fact he irritated me with his over-eagerness to please. His relationship with Jessie was another matter. 'The shagging sausages are burned,' I heard him shout at Jessie, for the hundredth time, one morning as he slammed out of the house. I knew that the longer they stayed the chances of Dad getting the upper hand were growing by the day. Derek was amazingly patient and said very little about how he felt about the situation, but I was aware that he was feeling the strain as the days went by.

'I'll find them a house,' I told Derek and he seemed relieved. How do you tell your parent that it is time for him to leave? Especially someone like Dad, an old-fashioned Irishman who believed that his daughter had a 'duty' to care for him in his old age – although at just forty-eight years of age he was anything but old. He had spent the last ten years or so working only when he felt like it, Maurice and Jessie being the main breadwinners. Jessie on the other hand was now getting too old to work, being nearly sixty. She was worn out and frequently not well. I saw the way the wind was blowing: Dad was working towards a situation where Derek and I would be his life support. This was not going to happen if I could help it.

'It was built for the shepherd, but he died,' Geordie McPhee, the factor for the Islay Estate, told me. I had by chance driven down the back road to Port Ellen the day before and spotted a newly built bungalow in the middle of a field. He handed me the keys so that Dad could view it. I kept my fingers crossed as

I drew a rough sketch for Dad, saying, 'It's just past the third cattle grid on the back road to Port Ellen.'

I told Dad that it was a wonderful chance for him to start again. There was plenty of work on the island for a decorator of his skill and I would help him to find jobs. This all appealed to him, and Maurice agreed to come to Islay and give him some help to get going.

Dad worked hard to get the bungalow decorated and furnished and I was delighted to hear him whistling in the morning, as he got ready to go off for the day. He was hopeful and looking forward to recapturing a life not unlike that of his youth in the Strawberry Beds in Dublin, when he had spent his days fishing and roaming through the countryside. He had no kids to worry about now and apart from Jessie, he had no responsibilities.

When they had settled into their new home Dad didn't need me, for the time being at least, and I was not surprised when he picked a row with me one day. I wasn't too bothered; the strain of having both him and Jessie plus the two dogs had dragged me down and a sort of gloom had descended on my home, and I was more than a little relieved to be free of him for a while. Of course, I didn't realise this until they had moved out. Dad had a way of creating a chilly atmosphere in a room without saying a word; it was just an expression on his face or a certain look in his very expressive eyes or the way he took deep sighs. My brothers had not been to visit while Dad was my lodger and I was glad. I had tried to get closer to Jessie, but apart from being grateful that I took the burden of cooking for Dad from her, she remained remote but polite; but she fell over herself for Derek, who treated her with kindness and respect. I don't know why, but I felt an extraordinary compassion for her. Not once, since I was about ten years old, had I seen her being hugged or comforted in any physical way. My training in psychiatry had focused in part on the importance of being loved and wanted. Dad and Jessie's relationship was unnatural and as unlike a loving partnership as it was possible to be. Of course, I hadn't seen Dad have any physical contact with anyone either. One night when he came to a ceilidh with us, he asked me to dance. I was astonished that he could dance, but it was embarrassing and awkward for us both to be in such close physical contact, and I think he was as relieved as I was when the dance finished. How different from the days long ago when I was a little girl, when I would sit on his lap while he helped me with my reading, or he would pick me up and twirl me high in the air making me squeal with the pure joy that Daddy was home. He had, however, no trouble at all cuddling his dog. The poor thing was old and sick and smelled terrible, but Dad didn't seem to notice. He obviously still had the capacity to love, but not, it seemed, anyone who could leave him or hurt him.

'All I want is to laugh and play music,' was Dad's constant refrain. He wanted a 'happy' home and why couldn't he have it? Could it be that it hadn't occurred to him that it takes two to make laughter – that all parties concerned must co-operate to create happiness and harmony. I think Dad thought that it had to be someone else's responsibility to make him happy. He expected to be treated with respect, but didn't show any to us or Jessie. When he was in a good mood the whole world had to respond likewise, never mind that he had been shouting and bawling five minutes before. Child-like, he couldn't understand why he was without his family. Conversely he was also capable of deep compassion and huge generosity, and he had an innate sense of justice – qualities I only recognised in him as I grew older.

I found the small-community mentality intrusive in the extreme. Everyone was related to everyone else somewhere on the island. When Dr Reid asked me to work for him, saying,

'Just a couple of hours a week would do,' he told me that it was difficult to maintain patient confidentially. 'They are all related to each other – it's a bloody nightmare,' he said, more to himself than to me.

Dr Reid's surgery was over on the extreme west of the island, in the enchanting village of Bruichladhie where he had been born and where his father had practised for more than forty years. When his father had died suddenly, Dr Reid had agreed to stay temporarily until a replacement could be found. It wasn't what he wanted to do; Gregory Reid had the makings of a brilliant career in paediatrics. Unfortunately the surgery was attached to his parents' house, and he felt that he couldn't have his mother looking for another home at her time of life. As is so often the case, Dr Reid did his duty and put aside his ambitions and hopes, and left the outcome to the gods. But he was not bitter. 'Ah, that a man's reach should exceed his grasp,' he quoted Browning, with irony.

The newspapers were always delivered a day late to the island, and not at all if the weather was too severe for the ferry to sail, and the bread was never fresh. A handful of families owned and controlled the majority of the retail outlets on the island and the cost of food was sky high. The local car dealer was David Monroe, a heavy thick-set man in his late forties. He sold only Morris thousands and if, as we did, you wanted a different make or model it could only be obtained by going to the mainland. He also owned the butcher's shop, as well as the only petrol station in Bowmore. Often he would hand a large parcel of meat to a customer who lived in the general direction of the Jura ferry and off-handedly say, 'Drop that off at the ferry.'

One Saturday, not long after we had arrived on the island, I was the chosen courier.

'I'm sorry, I'm not going as far as Port Askaig.' I told him that it would add another ten or twelve miles to my journey. A hush fell over the queuing women and I felt all eyes on me. I waited for my change, which he almost threw at me.

'It wouldn't take you but half an hour,' he accused me.

I didn't see why he should expect me to be an unpaid delivery driver, and as he didn't even take a couple of shillings off the very expensive meat he could take a running jump, and I told him so. I heard the collective sharp intake of breath behind me. These people were in the habit of being obliging and helpful to their own, and I admired them for that. But they couldn't or wouldn't see my point regarding this very rich businessman, that if everyone took my stance he would have been forced to employ a delivery driver. As I left the shop no one met my eyes. Before the door was properly closed behind me the excited babble started up. 'Typical of incomers!' I heard some old biddy saying.

Madge Morrison ran the clothes shop. I liked Madge, a small neat blonde woman, always perfectly made up, and whose expensive perfume delicately scented the little shop. She had a bright smile for everyone who passed through the portals of her empire. Thoughtful and discreet, if you tried on a beautiful dress you couldn't afford, she would say in a conspiratorial whisper, 'Pay me when you can, dear,' and she would carefully wrap the garment in tissue and brown paper. Being conscious that everyone went to the same events, she stocked only one of each style.

All telephone calls went through Jeannie, the woman controlling the exchange attached to her house at Port Ellen at the opposite end of Islay. You didn't need to know the number you wished to call.

'Hello, can you put me through to Dr Reid?' She didn't say, 'Certainly, madam': it was, 'Are ye no feeling well, graigh?'

133

and she would try to extract as much information of your condition as possible.

'No, Jeannie, I just want a repeat prescription.'

As she probably already knew why the prescription was needed in the first place, she would be satisfied and put you through. You had to hope that another caller kept her busy while you spoke to the doctor. If it wasn't the doctor she would sometimes break into the conversation to add her tuppence worth.

I found it frustrating that if I got up during the night someone would tell me that I had left a light on; did they ever sleep? The favourite topic of conversation was 'getting the peats in'; everybody appeared to own a peat furrow on the moors. At the WRI, or the Women's Royal Institute, a constant source of gossip was the quality of the neighbour's scones and heaven help the housewife whose washing was anything but sparkling white. It was definitely a matriarchal society. Two of the older men in the village would ignore each other until they were out of sight of their homes, then clatter through the village to the distillery together chatting companionably; their warring wives had forbidden them to be friends. I'm sure they had all forgotten what the row was about in the first place, but once a feud had started it went on for generations.

I found it difficult not to laugh when very late one night the policeman waved us down as we returned from a ceilidh on the other end of the island.

'Did you see another car on the road, Mr Stones?'

Derek told him that we had not seen anything at all. The policeman was very serious.

'There's been a hit and run.'

Naturally we were concerned and asked him if anyone was hurt.

Shaking his head and sighing deeply he almost whispered,

'Dead, I'm afraid.' He pointed to a dark heap lying next to a large gorse bush.

I jumped out of the car into the darkness to help and approached the 'body'. The policeman held his torch aloft, illuminating a very dead fat sheep. 'Hardly the crime of the century,' I muttered. There being little or no crime, apart from the odd poacher, this copper had very little to do and treated each 'incident' with due gravitas.

Donnie McLean was one such poacher, working, of all places, on the big estate. He seemed to have a knack for detecting – usually in the dead of night – 'diseased salmon', as he called them when caught by the gamekeeper. Archie Logan, the gamekeeper, supplemented his meagre income selling these 'deceased' fish to local hotels and amazingly he was always tripping over 'injured' deer on the road. The gun dogs on the estate had a disproportionate number of 'runts'; at £20 each, he accepted cash or cheques.

The managers of the distilleries were the overlords of their villages, being the highest-ranking officials of the companies that owned all the properties, including the houses, within each complex. Usually the manager's house stood apart from the rest of the workers' homes; in our village his house, a large white bungalow, was perched on a hill overlooking the rest of us. John Gilmore had been assistant manager when his old boss had died suddenly and tragically. Being in the right place at the right time, he secured the post of manager.

The stench from the draff (waste product from the whisky distilling process) hung over the village like a poisonous cloud. It had been heaped up at the back wall of the main warehouse and was rapidly forming a huge mountain. Eventually the older women of the village, led by the formidable Bella Dougan, couldn't stand having to keep their windows and doors shut tight and they stormed into John's office

like a gaggle of angry geese, demanding he get rid of it immediately. Our intrepid and very resourceful manager hit on a
brilliant plan.

Over the next couple of days a long parade of tractors and
trailers carried away mounds of the putrid mountain. The vile
stench wafted into every nook and cranny of the village, but
at last we were free to open our windows again. 'I warned him,
there's going to be bloody trouble,' Derek muttered. 'He's sold
that shit to the farmers without drying it first.'

The trouble wasn't long in coming. A few days later we
watched with a certain amount of vindictive glee as a succes-
sion of Land-Rovers and trailer-less tractors screeched into the
village looking for JG, obviously after his blood. The draff
having fermented in their stomachs, the cattle were falling
down drunk all over the place, keeping the vet busy and cost-
ing the farmers a fortune to boot in lost milk production.

Shuggie lived with his elderly mother on his farm a couple of
miles along the road from the village. I dropped in to see her
on my way home from the hospital one morning.

'She's failing fast,' Shuggie said as he walked me back to my
car. I had to agree. She was nearly ninety and had a bad heart.

'I think I should be looking for a woman, do you think?'

I thought he was thinking about a home help.

'No, I mean a wife it is I should be looking for.' I was a little
startled, but I told him that as he was still a relatively young
man in his early forties he would be a good catch for some
nice lady, perhaps in her forties too.

'Ah, but Mrs Stones, would they breed at that age?' He was
perfectly serious and couldn't understand why I was laughing.

'Shuggie, is it a woman you want or a cow?'

I left him scratching his head. He had been looked after by
his mother all his life and, with her death imminent, his need
for someone to look after him was uppermost in his mind;

love was not a consideration in his quest for a woman. I never found out if he managed to get a breeding woman.

Posters went up all over the island announcing a screening of a 'major feature-length film' to be shown at Bowmore Community Hall. 'Book early to avoid disappointment' the poster told us; I booked two tickets.

The packed hall waited expectantly and at last the lights were turned off. *The Hill* may have been a great film, but it lost something of its tension and drama when it kept breaking down. It continued to break down over the three-week period of the screening. I don't know if anyone on the island ever did get to see the entire uninterrupted 'full-length' viewing.

FOURTEEN

In the summer of 1973, I was thrilled when Derek applied for a job back on the mainland and was successful.

Before I left, I called on Jessie and told her to call me if ever she needed help.

'Don't worry about me,' she told me ungraciously. She appeared to have found a measure of happiness at last. Dad was being kept busy decorating one of the big estate houses near Port Askaig, and was developing a decent social life in pubs. He was hardly ever home and that suited Jessie perfectly. Her neighbours, who had a farm a little way down the road from the bungalow, provided her with some live chickens and ducks and she lavished all the love in her heart on them and the dogs. Dad had dug over a fair-sized garden for her and she was in her element. Maurice had left too, for which Dad blamed me. Now they had to stand on their own two feet. It was the first time since they had been together that they would be entirely alone.

I was looking forward to getting back to 'civilisation' and the luxury of being anonymous. But there were a few things I would miss about living on the island. The freshly caught flounders and mackerel bought from the young boys who speared the fish from the end of the little wooden pier. The ceilidhs, where I danced the Gay Gordons, Strip the Willow and the Eightsome Reel, fast energetic dances that left me breathless, especially if one of the young men of the island took me on the floor; often we danced till four in the morning. Rusty, the alcoholic dog who seemed to prefer my doorstep to sleep off the whisky he lapped up in the filling shed. He usually woke up snarling, his face screwed up and obviously suffering a hangover. The men thought it was funny; I thought they were cruel. Old Billy, who practised his bagpipes out at the end of the pier because everyone yelled at him to 'play far away'.

I would miss Yougan, the reclusive shepherd, who, with his brothers, sat on their mother's newly dug grave and finished several bottles of whisky to send her on her way to the hereafter. Occasionally he would wander down to the village and walk through the first door he found open, which one wet afternoon was mine. At first when I heard snuffling and snorting I thought a stray animal had wandered in. He was sitting on my cream sofa looking like a bundle of dirty rags and filling my living room with the most appalling odour. He didn't say anything – he didn't have to, as we all knew why he dropped in for a visit: he needed a 'wee dram'. Most of the people whom he visited would fill a small bottle with whisky and send him on his way. I poured a good measure of the finest malt and handed it to him. He swallowed it without a word and waved the glass in my direction indicating that another would be in order. Half an hour later I was relieved when Derek came home and Yougan left; not one word had he uttered during his visit.

I would miss Gordon the window cleaner, who saw nothing wrong in being probably the only window cleaner in the world who was afraid to climb a ladder. 'I can do your downstairs, hen. I don't go up ladders.' Fortunately he had no competition. I hired him for the novelty value. Derek grumbled that I was wasting money.

'You'll kill yourself one of these days, hanging out of the bedroom windows.' He didn't offer to do the windows, though.

I would miss the well-behaved and respectful children: Peter and Anne, Margaret's two; Findlay, a handsome little boy who lived two doors away and who was always willing to run an errand but refused to accept any reward; little Wilma, the painter's daughter, who was seven, so timid and shy but who protected her new baby brother like a little tigress, reminding me so much of me when I was her age ...

I would miss the safe security of this remote microcosm, the beautiful sunsets and the wild sea.

But unless you have been born to it, island life is something you enjoy far more when you have left it. I was glad to be leaving and as I watched Port Askaig disappear through the mist I felt relief and a certain excitement. Derek and I had attained a peace and companionship during our three years away from the stresses of the wider world. He had earned good wages as the engineer at the distillery and I had earned enough to cover the household expenses. In my mind we were just now starting on our married life 'proper'. My mind was at rest. My brothers were all on their way leading their own lives; yes, they would make mistakes, as we all do during life's journey, but they didn't need me now. Dad and Jessie were, as far as I believed, settled at last in a nice house and able to earn a decent living.

I hoped Dad wouldn't get it into his head to move again. It was his habit to move to a place that he happened upon, whether on holiday or just passing through – sometimes with disastrous consequences. Maurice told me that by far the worst time was when he rented a little weaver's cottage in a picturesque village in Yorkshire. He should have known that the cottage, the end one in a terrace of half a dozen or so, would have some problems when the landlord handed him the rusty six-inch-long key to the front door. 'Like a key to an ancient dungeon,' Maurice said.

Dad, enthusiastic as ever when he found somewhere new, said that all it needed was a lick of paint, and he and Maurice set to with a will. Maurice was pessimistically cynical that anything could make this old dwelling habitable. 'It didn't even have a bloody toilet, just a wooden hut at the end of the garden, practically in the field at the back of the house,' he told me as he related the story of the dreadful day the toilet almost collapsed around Jessie's head.

As Maurice and Dad were lining the front bedroom walls for the third time in the forlorn hope of keeping the damp at bay, they heard her voice faintly in the distance. 'Dessieee!' They didn't rush to answer her, but her calls became more urgent. At last they went out to the back of the house and to their horror they saw an enormous Hereford bull scratching its backside on the fragile rotting wall of the toilet. Jessie was trapped inside and the wooden structure was swaying alarmingly.

'Go and chase the fecking thing away,' Dad instructed Maurice, waving his hand wildly in the direction of the beast.

'You must be joking – look at the size of it!' Maurice was no fool; Jessie would be safe as long as the shed held up.

While they argued between themselves as to the best way to chase the bull away, Jessie could be heard talking calmly through the wall of the toilet to the beast, calling it 'girl'. Dad and Maurice thought it best not to tell her the full extent of her predicament. Maurice went for the farmer and by the time he had come back with him, the bull had walked serenely away and Jessie was having a mug of tea to calm her down; Dad had a large whisky.

Although they could all laugh about it later, I sincerely hoped there wouldn't be any more such adventures.

A sudden squall blew up, sending me scurrying below for shelter. The ferry rocked violently as it fought its way to the mainland. If I'd had a superstitious nature I would have taken the small storm as a bad omen. Can an optimist be pessimistic? Sometimes, maybe, but not me: my cup was always half full. Derek's was always nearly empty.

FIFTEEN

On arrival back on the mainland Derek and I bought our first house from the New Town Development Corporation, with a 100 per cent loan. Livingston was one of a number of new towns incorporated to ease the housing burden on some of the large cities. They were generally situated on some bleak moor twenty or so miles from the city. Livingston was almost halfway between Glasgow and Edinburgh. At first, families willing to move out of Glasgow were given the not inconsiderable sum of £500 in cash, plus moving expenses. It was a bleak place, with vast expanses of green, but not the mellow green of Ireland; these areas were dotted with clusters of mostly greyish pebbledash plain houses. Streets had glamorous names such as Heatherbank, Elm Grove or Spey Drive. A tiny shopping mall held the doctor's surgery, a butcher's shop, the Co-op, an estate agency and, most importantly of all for some of the residents, a solicitor's office. The population was constantly on the move, most of them going back to the tenements and slums of the city. There was no 'heart' in Livingston and I didn't blame them. But I was happy enough; I worked all the hours I could, frequently doing two shifts on the buses, although I didn't find the same fun and camaraderie this time round as I had years before in Oldham. I had decided not to go back to nursing as the pay was appalling and we needed the money. My plan was that if we could save up enough and pay off our debts I could contemplate being a mother.

*

I was shocked at the changes that had taken place in the few short years we had been away. We may as well have been in the wilds of the desert in Timbuktu. On Islay we had only been able to get BBC television, and the reception of that was very poor, so apart from reading the odd Sunday newspaper, we were blissfully ignorant of the raging inflation gripping Britain. The feminist movement was demanding that men did their share within marriage, and women wanted equal pay, but I was happy to be treated like a lady. I am still enchanted when a man holds a door open for me and when a few years ago a workman wolf whistled at me I was thrilled to bits. Decimalisation of the currency had happened when I was on Islay. Being young we managed to adapt easily to the new money – in fact it was really quite easy, but old people found it confusing. Of course we all mentally converted 'pees' back to 'real money'. The Treasury let us keep our two bob bits and shilling pieces, but constantly reminded us that they were now 'ten pee' and 'five pee' respectively. Harold Wilson had got the mandate to join the EEC and we were now Europeans, but being the isolationist island race that we are, we clung doggedly to 'traditional' British ways and customs. But we had no conception of how it had affected prices. I didn't see what all the fuss was about; everything had been expensive on Islay.

'We can't afford one now. Anyway, what do you want a kid for?' Derek said when I broached the subject with him and that was the end of the discussion as far as he was concerned. How can the need for a child be explained to a man? A deep primeval need stirred in me. I felt incomplete; there was someone missing. I had a recurring dream of a little boy who called out for me. I was deeply angry with Derek. But I felt sure that I would be able to change his mind sooner or later and dropped it.

We could, however, afford a new colour television, and a

shag-pile carpet; trying to keep the pile from resembling a dead, crazy-patterned sheep drove me mad. As the months wore on, it became obvious that Derek had no intention of ever fathering a child; he was thirty-three now and was happy the way things were. All his needs were attended to and he didn't have to put a lot of effort into our marriage.

One day I noticed a police recruitment poster on my bus and decided then and there that if I was not going to be a mother I would start a new career. Naturally Derek was opposed, but I held my ground. 'I'm joining the police and that's the end of it,' I told him.

Of course I had several hurdles to get over first, not least the entrance exam. I didn't realise how much I wanted to join the police until the morning of the entrance exam. All I could manage by way of breakfast was two cups of tea and several cigarettes. I nearly walked away from the police headquarters; I was overcome with panic. I pulled open the heavy door to the lecture hall bearing a large sign that said 'EXAMINATION IN PROGRESS' and joined fifteen other hopefuls, all men, in the large room. I stared at the paper before me and my mind froze.

'If it took six men three hours to dig a hole ten feet square and six feet deep, how long ...' The question even mentioned that one of the men spent a considerable amount of the time leaning on his shovel. 'Why would I need to know that?' I wondered in impotent rage. I hadn't a clue whether it was algebra, calculus, geometry or plain arithmetic. My maths teacher at school had spent three years trying to teach us algebra but I couldn't get the hang of it no matter how hard I listened; in fact I never even found out what it was or its purpose in the grand scheme of things. To my enormous relief the next page consisted of a speech some academic had given at a conference and the questions asked us to explain in plain

English what she had been talking about; that gave me no trouble. Some geography and multiple-choice questions completed the paper. I was not confident. Apart from my nursing exams, which gave me very little trouble, I had not had to put my very meagre education to the test. Secondary modern schools had been part of a tripartite system of grammar, secondary modern and technical set up in the 1944 Education Act, when education was thought to be 'essential' in the reconstruction of Britain when the fighting was over. Entry was usually by way of the eleven-plus examination but I arrived in the school system too late to take the eleven-plus. Having left school just before I was fifteen, I had taken no other exams.

Later the recruiting sergeant told me that I was in the top five of the candidates who had sat the exam with me. I was delighted.

'I, Evelyn Stones, hereby do solemnly, sincerely and truly declare and affirm that I will faithfully discharge the duties of the office of constable.' I was in front of a Justice of the Peace, holding a red leather-bound Bible and repeating the words after the fat, red-faced man, being sworn in to the police force. It was a very solemn occasion and reinforced for me the enormous commitment I was making in joining the police; it was almost religious.

I loved my new career from the moment I drove like a lunatic up the wide sweeping drive of the castle of Tulliallan, the police training college, and skidded to a halt in front of the imposing entrance. I knew I was late and, panting like a dog on a hot day, I asked where I should go.

'You're about twenty years too early for this end, hen,' the uniformed commissioner informed me and directed me to the junior college.

I joined the other new recruits, most of whom were

between eighteen and twenty years of age. As we assembled on the parade ground in our new uniforms and shiny shoes, I felt I belonged.

During the next six weeks we learned the basic knowledge required to patrol the streets, protect life and property, prevent and detect crime, and be impartial.

We learned that the public were lieges and articles produced in court were productions. Everything had a definition. Immigrants were 'aliens' and the Irish were 'the largest ethnic minority in Britain', who, apart from 'their happy-go-lucky fighting reputation, had generally blended quite well into British society'. Why the whole class looked at me at this point I don't know. We were made aware that we too were 'lieges' and could be offended as easily as anyone else, for the purposes of an arrest.

'For God's sake, constable, I am on your side,' poor Sergeant Campbell roared at me in his broad Highland singsong accent. 'You can nae lock a man up for saying "effing". Now what exactly did the accused say?'

We were learning how to give evidence in the court mock-up. I was trying to get a conviction for a breach of the peace. The 'fuck' word was a word that I found extremely offensive and I refused to say it in these circumstances.

'I promise, sergeant, I will say it in real life,' I assured him sincerely and he gave up on me. As it happened I never had to say that word once in all the times I took the witness box.

Being at the police college was as I imagined a posh boarding school would be. As soon as you entered the gates you were in a cocooned world with your own people. A quiet peace settled around you. Vast, beautifully manicured lawns dotted with glorious flowerbeds surrounded the ancient castle standing silent and watching the comings and goings of ages. Everything required was provided, right down to our black tights. All the tutors were sergeants and the only civilians were the domestic staff and the doctor from the local village who came and gave us a lecture on delivering a baby. I silently prayed I would never need the services of some of my male colleagues if their reaction was anything to go by. Several ran from the hall; a couple more literally fainted and slid under their seats. Some of the girls were not much better and I heard someone mutter, 'Christ, how disgusting!' There was a shudder in her voice. I didn't blame her really: the film of the birth we saw was very old, the doctor was wearing a red rubber apron and the only equipment visible was a very large Belfast sink. The mother in question had obviously given birth many times, as the one we witnessed practically fell out.

Friday afternoons were a trial for me, though. Sergeant Mc'Goven tutored us on the Road Traffic Act. 'Motor vehicles includes all mechanical propelled ...' He had a low droning monotone voice, and sitting in the warm classroom at the end of a week filled with three-mile runs, circuit training and parade square exercises I was generally very tired. I had no interest whatsoever in vehicles, their classification and whether they were fit for the purpose for which they were intended; my interest lay in child protection and vice. I usually had great difficulty keeping my eyes open, and often drifted off to sleep, only to be woken by the sharp elbow of my neighbour. All I really came out of that class with, at the end of the first six weeks, was how to remember which animals were covered by various pieces of legislation. All I had to remember was 'How Can A Motorist See Good People Die', as the capital letter of each word related to an animal – 'Horse, Cow, Ass, Mule, Sheep, Goat, Pig and Dog'.

It was at the police college that I met Shiona, who was to become my friend and remains so to this day: she's the sister I never had. I'll never forget her oration at the end of our course when we all had to speak for five minutes on any subject. I chose 'Man's inhumanity to our best friend, the dog', which went down like a lead balloon. Shiona's subject was the phrase 'You know'. It was hilarious, you know.

'Remember, lads, women are like chickens: the white meat is the best.'

I didn't think his feeble joke was funny and told him so.

'WC Stones has no sense of humour,' he announced sarcastically to the now silent class.

A few embarrassed titters broke out at that even more feeble remark. Over the course of my career I would often be addressed so. But as they say, 'Sticks and stones ...' The class were waiting for a retort in response; I let it go.

I had got off on the wrong foot with the person who had the power to pass or fail me at the end of the course. Classes with this instructor became a battle of wills between him and me. He was arrogant, chauvinistic and insufferably conceited, as were most of the younger instructors. I refused to laugh at his 'witty' repartee because it wasn't funny and I didn't rise to his baiting of me.

The day of our final appraisal was hot and sunny and Sergeant Blair took the class outside. A few of us were sitting under an enormous oak tree on one of the beautiful lawns in front of the castle. Three or four of the Commandant's peacocks strolled gracefully around us. Some of the male members of our class were throwing a ball around, some paced alone, but most sat in little knots nervously awaiting the call to the other side of the lawn to hear Sergeant Blair's verdict on our performance. Some of my friends were teasing me. Everyone expected that I would get annihilated in my appraisal. I was a little apprehensive, but there was nothing I could do to redeem myself.

Jan McGilvery was beaming when she rejoined us. 'He's no a' that bad.' She had done better than she had expected; I was happy for her. 'He wants you next, Evvy.'

I took a deep breath and strode confidently towards him.

'Ah, Evelyn, sit down.' It was the first time he had used my Christian name. I couldn't decide if it was a good thing or not. I braced myself and took the vacant chair facing him, carefully smoothing my skirt and crossing my ankles neatly.

'Don't look so worried,' he said. I smiled weakly at him, wishing him to get on with it.

'We've had our differences, but I firmly believe that you have the makings of a damn good police officer.'

I said nothing; I was not sure how to respond to this sudden, unexpected praise from him. I waited for the 'but'; it didn't come. Apparently I had 'leadership' qualities, could 'react' to situations in a mature and responsible manner and was capable of taking 'control' in a crisis.

We passed out in front of the top brass of the college, the inspectors, whom we hoped we wouldn't have to see, and the Director of Junior Training, also known as 'the digit', who held the rank of Chief Superintendent. Taking the salute was our dear Commandant, a retired army colonel, who had danced with me the night before at our end of course party.

'Ladies,' he grunted in my ear, 'should be the four Ps, what? Pretty, pink and permanently pregnant.' He roared, laughing at his own chauvinism.

I smiled politely; the man was a dinosaur, and I thought, Yes, you're the four Rs: ridiculously rotund, ruddy and rude.

Sergeant Kernan had done his best to teach us to march for this passing-out parade, where we stood smartly to attention, proud, eager and shining. I would challenge anyone to try to march to Herb Alpert and his Tijuana brass, especially if a stray peacock happened by and appeared to be more in step with the music than we were. It was over and we said our goodbyes. As the police motto said, 'Biglic-Biglic': 'Be wise, be circumspect'. We stepped out confidently, wise and circumspect. How many would last until the next year, when we would meet again for the three-month final course, I wondered.

SIXTEEN

I recognised poverty's malevolent stench immediately I stepped into the dingy hallway. The odour of unwashed bodies fought to overpower the rival stink of a very old, greasy chip pan, a mangy dog, urine and stale ashtrays.

Ginny Clarke struggled to focus her badly swollen black eyes. 'He didn'ne mean it, hen,' she told me, again trying to defend the brute who had given her yet another savage beating.

In the three months since I had been stationed at the new town, Ginny had become one of my 'regulars'. With depressing regularity Ginny's neighbours were forced to call the police when her screams pierced the night.

'You have to let me charge him, Ginny. He'll kill you one of these days,' I implored her.

But Ginny only wanted me to keep him out of the house until he sobered up. Her husband had usually fled by the time we reached her anyway.

Ginny had met Peter Clarke when her first husband had been killed in a road accident. She had had it all: a beautiful home, two lovely boys and a loving husband who provided well for his family. It didn't take long for Peter Clarke to squander the insurance money. Ginny started to join her new husband on drinking binges to dull the pain and humiliation of her reduced circumstances and very soon she lost her home. She lost sight of her sons' needs and she lost her sons too; the social services took them into care.

I looked round the dismal room, devoid of any comfort. The chair that she was huddled in was of indeterminate colour, the arms black and shiny with years of grime. A small, filthy, red Formica-topped kitchen table littered with old fish-and-chip papers, an overflowing ashtray, empty Carlsberg Special lager cans and a half-full bottle of Lanlic fortified wine standing under the window and an old television sitting on a few house bricks were all the furnishings in the room. There were no pictures, ornaments or even a mirror. A dim, bare bulb hanging from a dirty wire struggled valiantly to illuminate the whole room. Ginny was in her forties but looked nearer to sixty and as I looked at her thin, battered body I felt deep anger towards her husband, overwhelming pity for her and frustration that she felt unable to accept help.

'What's the use, hen? I'll be dead soon enough and nothing will matter.' There was no emotion in her voice; she was totally defeated and her spirit broken.

'She must love it,' some of the younger lads at the station would say when their efforts to charge violent husbands, sometimes even sons, were frustrated by the victims.

How do you explain to people who have never had to live with domestic violence how destructive it is – how it creates a total lack of self-esteem and an inability to see beyond the next beating? Often, women would blame themselves for having provoked the violence. 'It's my own fault, I was winding him up,' I often heard from them when they would refuse to press charges. Almost without exception the men involved were bullies, cowards and full of self-pity.

'She made me do it,' was the frequent reply to the charge of assault on the rare occasions we were able to get the necessary evidence.

Erin Pizzy, a brave and outspoken journalist, took up the cause of 'battered' women in the early seventies and opened the first refuge in 1971. But they were few and far between and, disgracefully, relied on public donations.

I was totally wrapped up in my job and didn't give a thought to much else. I spent more time with my assigned partner Bill than with Derek. Derek was more than happy that I had a career that I enjoyed. I was far more easy-going than I had been, and as much as possible he helped about the house when he could. My being out of the house so much meant that he could lie on the couch and watch as much football and cricket as he wanted. He wasn't concerned that I worked with so many men; he trusted me completely and I gave him no cause for concern, unlike a few of my colleagues. The men on my shift teased us unmercifully but we laughed it off with clear consciences; our relationship was close but always strictly professional and as such we were a good team.

I was fond of all my shift mates.

One of these was Sandy, who ran the tea fund and spent more time chasing the staff for their £1 a week contribution than on police work. He was a ruddy-faced, tall man with a shock of red, curly hair and he was just bumbling his way through the last ten years of his thirty years' service. He would retire on a full pension while he was young enough to enjoy it and he couldn't wait. One day Sandy had to deliver a message to a woman that her husband had just died in hospital and he asked me to accompany him. Using the occasion to give me some 'on the street' training, he explained the procedure for such times. 'Now, don't ask her if she's the widow McLean,' he instructed me. I didn't know if he was serious and, still stinging from my introduction to Mr Higginbottom at the mill, I said nothing.

As we walked up the path through the very neat little front garden, Sandy removed his hat, as was the custom on these occasions.

'Oh God! It's my Jimmy,' the middle-aged woman whispered when she saw us on her doorstep. We managed to catch her as she staggered back into the hallway. I soon learned to adjust my expression when calling on law-abiding citizens; in those days a visit by the police in most peoples' minds meant bad news.

Big John McFarlane was over six feet seven, but nonetheless a gentle giant until roused to anger. His pet hate was the 'smart arse' lippy motorist who was 'a good friend of the Chief Constable'. Our chief must have been a very popular man if the number of his 'friends' was anything to go by.

Jock Turner, one of our inspectors, an ex-army man, never tired of telling us about his service in India. 'You could smell Calcutta two days out to sea.'

One day dear Sergeant Douglas, who was in charge of our shift, or Dougle as we referred to him, sent me out to round up stray dogs, following numerous complaints from the residents of one particularly notorious estate. He was of course unaware that I had been (and still am) terrified of strange dogs ever since I had been badly bitten by Rex in Fatima Mansions when I was a child. To my eternal shame all I managed was one darling little puppy who ran to me wagging his tail; I 'huckled' him. Sergeant Douglas was not even slightly amused.

One Tuesday night, as Bill and I headed back to the station to hand over to the night shift, the radio burst into life.

'Foxtrot control, over.' The operator was calling for a crew to attend a 'domestic'.

Nobody responded; domestics were notoriously difficult to deal with. Often the parties involved would be laughing and joking with each other by the time the police arrived, claiming 'a little misunderstanding', and another two hours would be added to your day.

'Foxtrot control, over!' The controller was getting tetchy; she was tired too. It had been a very quiet shift and we had been reduced to harassing motorists.

Reluctantly I lifted the microphone and we were directed to an address near by. As we pushed the heavy glass doors to the six-storey block of flats there was no sound to be heard. Even the neighbours who had reported the disturbance were nowhere to be seen.

'Good, it looks like it's all over,' I said to Bill as we mounted the concrete stairs to the second floor. The door opened a crack as I pressed the bell. There was no reply but we could hear someone inside. I called, 'Hello, police,' and I pushed the door wide open.

'Jesus Christ!' It was an involuntary cry. There were pools of blood on the floor of the hallway and bloody hand marks along the walls. I heard a faint groaning sound coming from behind a door just inside the hall door. Careful not to step in the blood, I opened this door and saw a woman lying face down in a bath full of cold water. The back of her head was wide open and pouring blood, giving the appearance that she was in a bath of blood. I held her head above the water as Bill attempted to grab her husband as he jumped out of the living-room window. The CID took over the investigation. I went in the ambulance with Annie Blair and Bill made a start on the report. We didn't get home until after eleven o'clock the following night; Derek caught me as I fell asleep walking upstairs to bed.

Six months later Annie stood in the witness box at the High Court and told the judges that she had fallen and that her husband, John Michael Blair, a violent and notorious criminal, had only been trying to wash the blood off her head. Case dismissed.

Later I saw her trying to smoke a cigarette in the pouring rain. Her badly bleached blonde hair was plastered to her head, the long jagged scar clearly visible.

'You know, Annie, next time we might take the long way round,' I said to her. She shrugged; she didn't really care if she lived or died. My anger and frustration boiled inside. I watched her husband as he swaggered towards us. Annie visibly tensed as he put his arm possessively around her shoulder; she was his property to do with as he willed. He should have been locked up for six or seven years for his attempt to murder her. He smirked at me as he guided Annie away.

A couple of years later he was jailed for ten years for a series of violent robberies and there was great rejoicing at the station.

Most of our 'punters' were small-time petty thieves and shoplifters. A lot of them weren't 'bad', just stupid, and often we shared a laugh with our regulars. One young bowsie, known to the police since he was about ten years of age, tried one day, as we had our tea break, to collect donations from us for a bogus 'heart attack fund', as he called it. He might have got away with it if he hadn't been shaking a stolen Barnardo's collection tin under our noses, complete with label and a photograph of an 'orphan'.

'Foxtrot control! Foxtrot control!' It was young Martin, our cadet, shouting through the station control radio. Built like a house, he was one of the sweetest young lads I had ever known. Not more than two minutes before, we had sent him to the shop for Irn Bru and chips. There was panic and distress in his voice, but we ignored him, thinking he was playing one of his pranks.

'For fuck's sake, control!' He was almost screaming now. At once we all jumped from our seats and raced to the front door of the station. Martin was bent over the quiet lifeless body of Murphy, one of our 'characters'. He had obviously dropped dead on the steps on his way into the station. It was his habit to see which policewoman was on duty and, depending on who it was, he would shout, 'What colour's your knickers today then, hen? You sexy thing!' To me he would politely ask after my health and chat about the weather. I had threatened him that I would lock him up if he asked so personal a question. I did, however, like the old fool, as did most of the rest of the station. Gently I guided Martin back inside and made him a cup of strong, sweet tea. He was shaking like a leaf; this was the first dead body he had seen. 'I didn't touch him, honest, Evvy.' That had never even crossed anyone's mind, and I told him so.

An hour or so later, when the rest of the team returned to the station, they ribbed Martin unmercifully. One wag told him to draw an outline of the body with the yellow crayon we used at road accidents. 'The CID will want to know exactly where he fell,' they told him. Murphy would have been the first to admit that he was no Adonis, but I think he would have taken great offence at Martin's interpretation of his dead shape.

About ten years later I learned that Martin and my sergeant driving instructor, Ian, had died instantly when a new patrol car they were testing lost control. I wept for the loss of such a bright light that had shone on me during my voyage through life; I asked Our Lady to look after them both.

For the most part, the petty criminal fraternity accepted our respective positions in the grand scheme of things. We were coming to the end of an age when most men would never dream of striking a woman, and the men on my shift made sure I was never in any danger. The public still held the police in high esteem and we were respected. The seventies was still an age of relative innocence and violence was not a part of everyday life. There was no hint that one day armed policemen wearing protective body waistcoats would be patrolling our airports. Or that race riots would ravage our towns and cities, drugs would be a blight on inner-city housing estates and ordinary citizens could expect to be victims of crime at least once in their lifetime. The main problem with youngsters that we had to deal with was the new craze of glue sniffing. One night I found a youth slumped on a stairway, completely befuddled. An empty crisp bag full of grey wood glue lay abandoned by his side. His mouth and nose were covered with the sticky substance. He was a big lad and Bill and I half carried, half dragged him to the car and took him home.

'Ye little bastard, ye,' his mother screamed at him. I watched, wide-eyed, as she removed her Scholl sandals, stood on a chair and proceeded to batter her son around the head with one of the wooden sandals, all the while telling him what his father would do to him when he got home. We never had any dealings with this particular youth again.

Parents for the most part would listen and take advice from the police then. There was still a certain stigma attached to the 'Polis' coming to the door.

For the first time in my entire life, I was completely happy and fulfilled. It seemed to me that nothing could spoil it.

SEVENTEEN

'Is that you, love?' It was the unmistakable voice of Jessie and she was obviously distraught. My heart pounded. Why was she calling me? Had Dad died, or was someone in trouble, I wondered? She said nothing for a long few seconds.

'Is anything wrong?' I squeaked into the mouthpiece, anticipating trouble. It was difficult to understand what she was saying through her tears. I had only seen Jessie crying once before and I was alarmed. All I could make out was 'fancy woman' and 'ducks'. 'He said I could be his house-keeper.' The line went dead.

I decided to call Jamie Logan, whose farm was just along the road from Dad's house. It was he who had given her the ducks and chickens on which she poured all her love, and Jessie had made friends with him and his wife before I had left the island. I was praying that Dad hadn't fallen out with him as he had done with nearly all the neighbours he had lived beside over the years. I hoped Jamie would be able to shed some light on the strange conversation I had just had with Jessie. I didn't want to risk calling her at home in case Dad was there.

'Hiya, Jeannie. Would you get me the number of Logan's farm on the Old Glen Road?' I allowed Jeannie to interrogate me for a couple of minutes before putting me through.

'Jamie, I hope you don't mind me calling you.' I knew Jeannie was still listening; I set the trap. 'Dad's phone line seems to be out of order.' Quick as a flash Jeannie broke in and told me that she would see to it right away.

'It's all right, Jeannie, leave it for now. Thank you, cheerio.' She understood by the sharp tone of my voice that I wanted privacy and sure enough I heard the click which told me that she was off to tune into someone else's business.

'Jamie, is there anything wrong with Jessie? She seemed very upset when she called me a few minutes ago.'

I heard Jamie sighing deeply and he paused slightly before he answered.

'Well, the rumour is that your dad has taken up with a widow woman from Bowmore and your mum has taken ill out of it.' He went on to tell me that he didn't want to be seen as poking his nose in, but Jessie had been saying strange things recently. 'I think she might crack up over it.'

I thanked him and asked him if he would try to get Jessie to his house in the next hour.

Jessie was still tearful when I spoke to her. ''E's going to marry that bitch.' As I listened to her despair, my heart bled for her. Although there was no love lost between her and my father, she couldn't imagine trying to start all over again at her time of life. ''E said I could be 'is housekeeper. I don't know what I'm going to do.' There had been times when I disliked my father or had been frightened by him – as when he had burst into my home on Islay, shouting and bawling and threatening to hit me because Maurice had left – but I never hated him. Now I felt loathing for the man who was prepared to discard a woman who had worked hard for nearly twenty years looking after him and, yes, to a certain extent, his children. He must have known that his pathetic offer to have her as his housekeeper would be refused. Maybe he thought that, had she accepted, it might salve his conscience. Poor Jessie, I couldn't imagine how she was feeling, but she was badly affected.

'You can come and stay with Derek and me,' I told her. I

could have bitten my tongue out as soon as I heard myself saying it, but I couldn't turn my back on her. I told her I would call her the next day, which I did.

'Just take the essentials. Yes, you can bring Soldier. No, leave the ducks and chickens. Jamie will take them along to the farm when you're gone.' I had a difficult time persuading her that she could get away and that she could start again. 'You just can't stay there in that situation,' I told her. I knew I could get her a pensioner's bungalow from the New Town Development Corporation; they were trying to populate the town and as my 'mother' she was entitled to be housed. 'Maurice will meet you at the other side, so make sure you're on that ferry,' I warned her. I told her that he would be driving five hundred miles from Berkshire. I was glad that Maurice had decided not to go over to the island; there would have been murder for sure.

Not long afterwards I saw a large, moth-eaten fur coat walking up my footpath and as I went to meet it I saw Jessie hidden inside. She didn't resist when I held her tightly for a long moment, and as I led her into my warm and cosy home, I saw silent tears wetting her thin, haggard face. Her grumpy spaniel followed closely at her heels.

'What are these for?' I had decided to go through the vast array of little brown tablet bottles neatly lined up on the dressing table.

'For my blackouts.' She had managed to convince the doctors on Islay that she suffered from epilepsy and was taking quite large doses of phenobarbitone, along with an assortment of painkillers and God knows what else.

I put the lot down the toilet and made an appointment for her with my own doctor. Years later, when Dad told me that she had frightened the 'bejasus' out of him and had gone 'off her rocker', I realised immediately why. Phenobarbitone has a powerful effect on the brain.

The doctor showed me the X-rays. 'She has a significant carcinoma on her right lung, but it's operable.' I was not too surprised; that hacking cough of hers had got worse over the years and she was now just a bag of bones. But she was clinging doggedly to her opinion that she was in possession of only one lung.

'Jessie, I have seen the X-rays and you have definitely got two lungs.' It was exasperating.

She had been with us for a couple of months and was no trouble at all. In fact, she took it upon herself to do the housework and washing and was happy as long as she didn't have to cook or go shopping. However, I had to prepare her for independent living and she was dreading it, I knew. Outside the house she became a quivering wreck. She seemed relieved that she had a serious illness. With Derek's help I finally persuaded her to have the life-saving operation. She was in hospital for nearly six weeks before they would operate on her; she had to be weaned off the cigarettes and her strength built up. All the attention and being looked after by the hospital staff brought her to life and I saw the lights come on in her eyes.

The hurricane that swept Britain in 1976 on my birthday, 2 January, killed twenty-two people. It was to be a year of extremes in every sense, not least for me.

Jessie made a swift and remarkable recovery from her operation.

As I approached the recovery ward one of the nurses had told her she had a visitor and I heard her say, 'That'll be my daughter.' I thought there was a modicum of pride in her voice. 'Get me my teeth quick! I don't want 'er to see me like this.'

That was a strange thing for her to say. Not only was it the first time she had referred to me as her 'daughter': I had seen Jessie in all sorts of conditions and why it would matter to her if I saw her *sans* teeth was a mystery to me.

When she saw me, she said, 'Oh, it's you,' disappointment evident in her voice.

I put this extraordinary exchange down to the effect of the anaesthetic. I didn't for one second think that Jessie had had a change of heart about me. I was certain that she still secretly harboured ill feeling towards me; on several occasions I had overheard her running me down to Derek.

While she convalesced in our home, I approached the New Town Development Corporation for a house for her. Within a matter of weeks Jessie was allocated a two-bedroom house a few minutes' walk from our street, in a small development built along the lines of a Spanish village. There were little alleyways and unexpected squares, and the houses were painted in scorching terracotta, dazzling white and sunny yellow. Unfortunately, in placing such an ambitious and brave scheme in one of the coldest and wettest parts of Britain, it didn't quite work the way the planners had envisaged it. Later on, the estate became crime-ridden and one of the most notorious hangouts for the local yobs, who had many escape routes through the warren of passages and alleyways.

Nevertheless Jessie was delighted with her new home and in particular the fact that she was free to do exactly as she wished. She had done it! She had started a new life. I felt the burden lift from my shoulders.

To say she was a burden is a little unfair. She had tried to be the perfect guest and kept to her room as much as possible, which made me feel guilty, and she made no demands on either me or Derek.

I was tolerant of Jessie, having nursed a great many elderly patients. I knew how difficult they could be, and she was anything but difficult.

*

While I looked after Jessie, though, generally adult children were now too busy leading their own lives to be closely involved with elderly parents. The days of the extended family had gone. Inflation was out of control and interest rates were sky high, forcing many women to work full-time, if they could get a job in the first place: unemployment had reached a record one and a half million. In the old days most married women would stay at home and look after the family. Children now got used to caring for themselves after school; the 'latchkey kid' was born. Parental discipline was becoming non-existent and 'yob culture' was in its infancy. A new mood of belligerence became apparent.

I was shocked into anger when one night Bill and I were called to deal with a gang of youths who had gathered outside a house, harassing a woman as she sat by her mother's deathbed. 'Fuck off, pigs,' one of them screamed at us as they insolently strolled away. Well, I was one of the 'lieges' and I was deeply offended; we arrested him. His father said in the most condescending way, 'My dear young woman, my son would never behave that way. Why don't you go after some real criminals?' I felt that he had almost patted my head; he wasn't going to discipline the boy. I decided to charge his darling son with a breach of the peace.

The Procurator Fiscal asked me to tell the court exactly what the defendant had said.

'He told me to eff off, Your Honour,' and I added demurely that he had said the whole word. He was fined £15 with time to pay; his daddy glared at me and paid the fine on the way out.

The expression 'neighbours from hell' had not entered everyday usage. We did have such people but they were few and far between, and generally they were warring married couples screaming at each other. Generally, a quiet word from the police achieved the desired effect for the neighbours. But there was one character who found it impossible to understand that his lifestyle was badly affecting all those around him in a small block of flats not far from the police station. Willie Patterson was stone deaf and the proud owner of a deep bass voice that sounded like Donald Duck with a sore throat. In his late sixties, he was completely toothless and his complexion was that of a beetroot. His face was lopsided as a result of a stroke he had suffered a few years earlier. The general view of Willie among my shift mates was that he was as bright as a ten watt bulb but completely harmless, and we were fond of him. He was a regular visitor and we all helped him to fill out his numerous official benefit forms. He had what today is referred to as 'learning difficulties'. Willie lived his life out of kilter with the rest of the world and often treated the middle of the night as midday.

That summer was the hottest recorded since 1772 and must have sapped the strength of the criminal fraternity; we had a very quiet time. With a certain amusement we wondered what the new Minister of Drought could do to bring rain. Water supplies dried up in some parts of England, and standpipes were installed in the streets of Yorkshire.

When I joined the force there was a 'women's' department. We were paid 5 per cent less salary than the men. We didn't mind at all. We didn't attend rough incidents like pub brawls. We didn't have to stand for hours directing traffic on cold road junctions and we definitely didn't do night shifts. Some of the older policewomen had never even attended any incident during the entire course of their service; they did office duties or stood quietly beside female prisoners being questioned by their male colleagues and carried little children to police cars.

Without consulting us – and why would it? – the government decided that we should have equal pay. That was the law for all other sectors of industry after all, but the condition was that we join the main body of the force and carry out the same duties.

'Jim,' I said through gritted teeth during a heated debate in the tea break. 'If I get 5 per cent more in my pay packet, will you get five per cent less than you get at the moment?' Some of the older hands resented the fact that they would now have to work with 'dollies', but they kept their counsel. Jim had been in the force for less than six months, having been demobbed from the army after nine years' service, and this service counted towards his police pension. He had an opinion on everything, a big mouth, and was still stuck in the past as far as career women were concerned.

'That's not the point.' He was shouting now, always a sign that an argument was being lost and getting out of control.

I got up to leave and as I reached the door I heard the policewoman from his shift say nastily, 'I don't know what the force is coming to when they let common bus conductors in.' I fled in tears, wondering if that was the general opinion. For a brief moment my happiness was blighted.

Superintendent Jean Cunningham summoned me to police headquarters. Every man in the force was terrified of her. She had a reputation that was equal to that of any hard man and was fearless in her dealings with anyone, criminal or constable.

'Sit, lass, there's nothing to worry about.' Jean Cunningham saw the policewomen as 'her girls' and resented the fact that we were now under the control of station inspectors, in practically all cases men. She had fought tooth and nail to keep her girls' department intact. She kept a close eye on us all, visiting the county stations and knowing full well that she had the rank to ensure that we were being treated well. 'Some of my girls look grey and tired,' I heard her say once in a very sharp tone to Inspector Turner. She went on to tell him that she held him personally responsible for our welfare and well-being. I don't suppose she realised that she was perpetuating the myth that we were delicate flowers unequal to the task of fulfilling our role alongside the men. She meant well, but she was in her own way a dinosaur.

I waited while she lit a cigarette and ordered a pot of tea via her intercom.

'Now then, Evelyn, the college need female instructors and more than that they need mature female instructors.' She paused to sip her tea. I wondered what was so frightening about Jean Cunningham. She was a tall, large-boned woman and obviously strong-willed, but that came from long years of service, an absolute belief in herself and supreme confidence that no one could tell her how to do her job. Jean had seen and done it all; she had the respect of her colleagues and she knew it. She had something that I recognised in myself: she told it how it was. She had no idea how to be political. She had no need to be. I could well see how as she progressed in what had been a small, county force, the 'old guard' would have seen her as an asset to the top ranks; she was dedicated, efficient and fearless, and had no intention of getting married.

'How long have you been married now, Evelyn?' I didn't see what that had to do with anything but I told her. 'Nearly ten years, ma'am.'

'Are you planning to have children?' How could I tell her that I would have loved to have had a child but my husband didn't want any.

'It didn't happen for us, but now I have my career and I don't suppose it will happen after this length of time.' I gave her the most honest answer I could. I didn't want to appear disloyal to my husband. I knew there was no chance of Derek changing his mind about children, and in any case I wasn't too bothered now. We didn't even discuss it any more.

Jean went on to tell me that I was to be stationed at head-quarters at the end of the year, where I would be coached in the exams necessary for qualification to teach at the police training college. I sat stunned for so long after she had dismissed me that it brought a sharp, 'Was there something else, constable?' from her. I snapped out of my chair and saluted her. 'No, ma'am. Thank you, ma'am.'

I hoped I sounded calm. I was on a cloud. In two years I would be back at my station with the rank of sergeant and could apply for the CID. I was on my way.

I tried to reassure Derek that he would hardly notice that I was not at the local station. 'I'll be able to come home three weekends out of four and most Wednesday afternoons. And it's only for two years.' I could see that he was not convinced. But I was not going to pass up the best opportunity I would ever have in my life. The police service was now my life and I was going to see to it that nothing would ruin it for me. My lack of education frequently caused me anxiety. Derek's job as manager of an animal feed company involved attending functions with his bosses from London and America, at which often I heard words during conversations that I understood only by analysing the context in which they were said. Although I was articulate and reasonably bright, I felt awkward and intimidated in the company of people who had been educated. I covered my inferiority complex by being as vivacious and witty as I was able; I didn't realise until many years later that this was all that was required of women in my position. Successful men generally had dim but decorative wives and I suppose the people Derek and I mixed with on these occasions thought I was one of these. Frequently they were amazed that I had a career of my own.

My ability to be vivacious on social occasions led to one of the worst rows Derek and I had had in a long time. One of his biggest customers asked him for a favour: 'Do you think I could borrow Evelyn for the farmers' annual dinner?'

What surprised me was that Derek didn't think to ask me if I would like to attend a grand dinner at the Gleneagles Hotel with someone I didn't even know. And he didn't think it was wrong of the man to ask such a thing. What enraged me was that he agreed to 'lend' me out for the night.

'You can take a bloody running jump,' I shouted at him. 'How dare you think that I am a thing to be passed along to your friends?' I was beside myself with rage.

Derek just didn't see my point. He was only doing a favour for a customer. 'Anyone would think I had asked you to sleep with him, for God's sake,' he shot back. He tried the 'help me out this time' routine. 'Look, you'll have a great time. I'll drive you there and pick you up. Please, I've promised him.' I told him to bugger off and suggested that he might make a better living as a pimp. Needless to say I didn't go on my 'blind date'; in fact I tried to avoid going to any function if at all possible, even swapping day shifts for nights with some of the men at the station, who were only too glad to oblige.

Police training college would teach me a whole new language and give me a range of knowledge that even a university education could not give: for instance, the definition of a 'pedlar' – which covered twenty different trades including 'a mender of chairs' or 'a petty chapman' – or what to do in the event of 'a major incident'. Would a university graduate know how to deal with an earthquake, for example? Not that there were many earthquakes in the Lothian Region. The police instructors would have a willing blank canvas with me and I couldn't wait.

I decided not to tell any of my colleagues why I had been summonsed to headquarters. I reasoned that the fewer people who knew of Jean Cunningham's plans for me, the less likelihood there would be of someone wrecking my chances; it was my secret and would remain so.

At last the rain came spilling out of the sky, signalling the end of the long hot summer.

'Well, that's you pregnant!' Derek said one night in October as he rolled over and reached for his cigarettes. Of course, I dismissed that from my mind. I had been on the Pill for only two of our ten years together and there had never even been a 'scare', never mind a positive result. I knew Derek still didn't want children; we hadn't discussed it for years and I had no reason to suppose that he had changed his mind. I had come off the Pill because of the scaremongering in the press about the long-term effects on women my age who smoked.

'Now is not the right time,' I told him. He didn't answer me. I fell asleep praying, like a million women the world over, for different reasons, 'Please God, don't let me be pregnant now.'

'Are you sure that was our last long weekend off?'

Bill and I were checking the duty sheet on the board.

'Of course I'm sure. That was the weekend you went to your niece's christening.' My brother Kevin and his wife Margarette had kindly asked me to be godmother to their firstborn and I felt both honoured and grateful – I would have been satisfied with being an aunt. 'Honestly, Evelyn, sometimes you have a head like a sieve,' Bill explained patiently.

Never one to mind the passing of time, I panicked. I had had a period on our last long weekend off; that much I was certain of. It had been my first since coming off the Pill. I decided to say nothing to Derek until I was sure.

I had a test and my hands shook as I dialled the surgery number to find out the result. The conflict in my mind threatened to overwhelm me. One half of me was desperate for a positive result and the other half was pleading for a reprieve. I weighed both possibilities. Surely in this day and age I would be able to continue with my career, although I was well aware that any notion of being an instructor at Tulliallan would definitely be out of the question. Could it be that Derek had deliberately got me pregnant? Surely he hadn't planned it? My thoughts wandered back to the summer and his constant concern that I would die if I didn't come off the Pill. I shook my head, denying to myself that he would go to those lengths to stop me going to the college. What if I was pregnant? Would I forgive him? Already in my mind I was angry and bitter that he could do this without discussion. On the other hand I should have been wise enough to guard my dreams and ambitions. I tried to imagine what it would be like to hold my own baby. I had held other people's babies and felt the pangs of longing. When I had to deal with a cot death I cried with the parents as I examined the tiny perfect baby for any sign of obvious injury. The howl of grief from a mother's heart at losing her newborn infant has no equal. Would I want to risk such heart-searing pain?

At last the receptionist answered. I waited impatiently whilst she rifled through files. 'Mrs Stones? Yes, the result is positive. Would you like to make an appointment to see the doctor? Hello ...'

Dazed, I had put the receiver down without thinking to say thanks or cheerio. I sat for a long while, trying to take in the consequences of my newly diagnosed condition.

The jarring ring of the telephone startled me.

'Evvy, are you coming in today?'

It was Bill; I had lost track of the time, but I wanted to be alone for now and told him that I had a bad headache. 'Make my excuses to Inspector Turner will you?' He knew there was something not right but I fobbed him off. Derek had the right to be the first to know that he was going to be a father, but for the moment I wanted to nurse this secret to myself and to be alone with my baby.

I drove my red Mini into Edinburgh and walked with the crowds along Princes Street until I found a shop I had never set foot in until now. As I paid for the whisper-soft tiny bootees, I knew then that I was truly going to have a baby, and an extraordinary joy settled on me. I called Derek from a telephone box and wept with joy as I told him the news.

'I know what you're going to tell me.' Superintendent Cunningham had her chin resting on her clasped hands and was looking me squarely in the eye. I thought I saw reproach and disappointment in her expression. 'Well, the first thing we must do is get you off the street,' she said as she lifted the telephone and asked her secretary to call Inspector Turner. I felt that I had let her and all my colleagues down.

'Don't be ridiculous, woman. If that's what you wanted, I'm delighted for you.' She was brisk but kind. I listened impassively as she barked down the line to Jock Turner. 'She must be relieved of street duty immediately.' She would let him know what was to be done with me after she had spoken to the Chief Super.

It was as though I had become invisible. I crossed my fingers, hoping that they would find something for me to do in the long months ahead.

Jessie said, 'Don't lift anything 'eavy, love, and drink plenty of cabbage water.' I had no intention of having cabbage water within a mile of me, but I smiled at her as she continued. 'If it's a lad you want then eat as much salty grub as you can, and sweets if you want a lass.' Poor Jessie and her old wives' tales.

Derek treated me like a fragile glass ornament and the men at work made me lots of cups of tea. I had been assigned to the Chief Superintendent's office in charge of juvenile liaison. It was better than having to resign, but I was bored being stuck in the office and haunted the Sheriff's Court next door where some of the old hands worked.

One day the court officer asked me to keep an eye on a prisoner awaiting trial. It was Pamela Farqhar, well known to me and every other police officer in the division. I was happy to oblige and took my knitting with me. I had decided to try my hand at knitting for my new baby. Apart from the time in the convent when I was taught to knit a sock, I had never held a knitting needle.

'You're never gonnae put that on a wean!' Pamela shot at me, having watched silently as I struggled with the tiny garment. Her tone was accusing.

I passed the knitting to her and was fascinated as the needles flew through the wool.

Pamela had spent nearly half of her fifty-two years serving short-term prison sentences. Unfortunately she had become institutionalised and as soon as she was released she would commit another crime.

One memorable Saturday she had walked into the station and emptied several large plastic carrier bags out on to the front desk.

'There ye 're, all chored, what ya gonnae dae aboot it?' she said proudly.

My shift mates ran for cover, and I looked in despair at her booty. None of the dozen or so shops I trailed round could say for certain that the goods I showed them had been stolen.

'Sorry, Pam, I'll have to let you go.'

She pleaded with me to lock her up. 'Look, hen, if I'm no back by ten o'clock on Monday I'll lose my job in the machine shop.'

It was to no avail. 'Pam, there is no evidence that the gear is stolen – you know that better than me. Now go away!' I sent her on her way with the stolen property, and went back to my tea. Less than ten minutes later a treble nine call was relayed to the station. We found Pamela sitting among the shattered large plate-glass window of the Co-op, which littered the path of the main street. A huge crowed of onlookers surrounded her and the brick she had used was clasped tightly to her chest.

'Oh, Pamela, what are we to do with you?' It was a rhetorical question. I knew exactly what she wanted me to do with her. And now I could oblige her.

'Just make sure I'm in front of yon daft Sheriff first thing Monday morn,' was her reply to the charge.

'Ye miserable bastard ye! That was worth six months at least,' she screamed at poor old Sheriff Findlay who kindly sentenced her to three months. I had to drag her out of the courtroom, still screaming her head off at the injustice of the miserly sentence.

But for all that, I was exceptionally fond of her. She had a keen sense of humour and a wicked wit. She was hugely amused at the ignorance of the younger generation, and the gullibility of a couple of the prison officers. 'I pretend to be holy, like, ye ken,' she told me, her eyes heavenward, meaning that she could get extra favours from one particular officer who was very religious. Many years before, she had been married and had lost the two children of her marriage to a blaze started by a chip pan. Her husband had fallen asleep having lit the cooker under the pan. 'I kicked the bastard oot; he burned my weans,' was all she would say about that part of her life; prison was the only home she knew after that.

A prison officer called a couple of days later and asked me if I would mind if the prisoners made the layette for my baby. Of course I didn't mind. 'We are going to have a raffle and the winner gets to make the christening robe,' she added. All I had to do was pay for the wool. It seemed that the prisoners were constantly battling boredom. I was thrilled and grateful.

I never did see the point of keeping women in prison. Apart from one or two exceptions they were not bad in the criminal sense. One poor woman was serving a life sentence for murdering her husband, a brute who had tortured and raped her over a period of fifteen years. When she could take no more, she had plunged a pair of scissors deep into his chest, piercing his heart and killing him instantly. 'It's worth it,' she whispered, when sentence was passed.

A few years later Pamela died as she would have wished, surrounded by the prison staff in the infirmary. Her funeral saw a large turnout of police and prison officers; Pamela Farqhar would have been satisfied that the only 'family' she had were praying at her graveside. I prayed that there was a machine shop for her in heaven.

Shiona and I were sent to England to collect a prisoner who had been arrested on warrant in Chester.

'Watch that one, she's wild,' the station sergeant told us as he led us to her cell.

Maggie Ingles was curled up on the filthy cot, sobbing her heart out. The sergeant left us to it, obviously glad to have been relieved of the responsibility of the 'wild Scotch' woman.

'They'll no' tell me where my weans are.' No wonder she was going mad. Her 'crime' had been failing to appear on a means inquiry warrant to answer charges of benefit fraud. She would not have been given a prison sentence for the actual fraud as it was her first offence, but she had incurred the court's displeasure in failing to turn up on the due date. She had left Scotland and didn't know that the court wanted to see her. When the police turned up at her door at dawn, always a good time to serve a warrant, and arrested her, she went berserk. They took her three children and didn't tell her where they had been taken. We were able to get the information and she settled down. The three of us had a bit of a laugh as we travelled back to Scotland on the train. Strangers would have taken us for friends on an excursion.

'A constable must discharge his duties according to the law, without fear, favour, affection, malice or ill-will' according to the lesson notes given to us at the start of our career. But one vital quality was missing from this directive: that of compassion. How can anyone charge an old lady, for instance, with shoplifting a small tin of John West middle-cut pink salmon, or a tin of Old Oak ham? We didn't discuss it, but I'm sure I was not the only one to have taken an old dear to her home for a chat and a cup of tea, and to have kept the 'evidence' in my locker before returning it to the shopkeeper. What was the point of snatching children from a deeply depressed mother, who couldn't be bothered to clean her home, didn't care where her children were or what they were doing, and was up to her neck in debt, when a call to the SSPCC would get her the help she needed to put her life back together again?

As much as possible we avoided using the fledgling social work department: we were distrustful of each other. That distrust was compounded one terrible week when a little boy's body was found in the river. All police leave was cancelled and we worked long hours doing house-to-house enquiries, and combing the riverbank for 'clues'. 'The killer has got to be found,' our Chief Superintendent ordered, quite needlessly; we were all of the same mind.

Three days later a young, middle-class woman social worker walked into the station. With a plummy voice and a matter-of-fact manner, she announced to the Inspector that she had been sheltering the killer for a few days to allow him to 'get over the trauma' of having strangled the child and dumped his little broken body in the river. She was extremely lucky not to have been charged with wasting police time. It seemed to police officers that social workers believed in protecting the criminal who had 'social problems' or was 'inadequate' or had 'had a deprived childhood' and therefore deserved not punishment but help, whereas police officers saw crime for what is was, a destructive and devastating intrusion into peoples' lives.

But I would miss it all: the camaraderie, the laughs, the tears, the satisfaction of having helped some unfortunate desperate soul to face another day. With great reluctance and sadness I hung up my hat. The formalities of resigning took me by surprise. In those days there was no such thing as maternity leave for women police officers; the worthies who had compiled the Equal Opportunities Act had exempted the armed forces and the police. I handed my uniform and warrant card into the clothing store at headquarters.

'I must have your whistle and epaulette numbers,' the efficient clerk told me. I enquired sarcastically if I was required to unsign the Official Secrets Act; unreasonably, I was angry with him. I was a civilian again, and a heavily pregnant one at that. Of course everyone at the station told me I would be welcome to drop by any time. But it doesn't work like that: ex-cops are the biggest nuisance imaginable to a working station. They have left the loop, as it were, and it is impossible to bring them into the circle of a discussion. The usual petty gossip at meal breaks means nothing to them. There's no sadder sight than a retired policeman hanging round his old station; he's just not wanted and he has become irrelevant. Studies at the time estimate that the life expectancy of a retired career policeman is only six years.

I examined the envelope, turning it over several times and trying to guess why a solicitor in Glasgow would be writing to me. 'McDonald, McBride and Pringle notaries SSC Writer to the Signet' informed me, 'We have been instructed by our client Mr Desmond Doyle to write to you regarding the whereabouts of Mrs E. Doyle.' It seemed that my father was trying to get divorced from my real mother in order to marry the widow from Bowmore. I was amazed at his gall. Had he telephoned me I would have considered helping him, but that would have meant him bending that stiff neck of his. He must have thought that I would be intimidated by a solicitor's letter and snap to.

Derek said I should help him. 'After all, he is your father and his treatment of Jessie was really nothing to do with you.' He added that maybe Dad had his reasons for behaving the way he did. 'You can't know what went on in their relationship.'

All I knew was that he had behaved in the most cruel fashion, and if he really had to have his 'widow woman', the decent thing to have done would have been to leave the bungalow and let Jessie keep her home at least.

'Christ! Evelyn, she hates you and always has, don't you see?' Derek said.

Yes, I did see, although I couldn't understand why she still had ill feelings towards me. I assumed that it was just a habit with her now. Maybe she resented having to rely on me. Perhaps she thought that if I had not continued to help her Maurice would have taken her in. Of the six of us, Maurice was the only one Jessie had convinced herself was her real son. Kevin and Dermot, my youngest brothers, were frequent visitors to my home and she went out of her way to avoid them. She had no time at all for Kevin's beautiful baby, Tracy-Jane, and was brusque and rude to Dermot's wife, Elsie, one of the sweetest women on this planet. I felt sorry for Jessie for missing the opportunity to have a real family life, which had been there for her if she had wanted it. Many times I have been asked why I persisted in trying to be a daughter to her at this time; the answer is that I honestly don't know, but maybe I was feeling guilty for the terrible life she had endured with my father. It has never been a chore for me to be kind to old people, especially those who have had a really hard life, as so many of Jessie's generation had.

But it never ceased to amuse me how Jessie kept up the pretence of liking me. She insisted on helping me with my housework and little jobs in the garden. 'You 'ave to watch yourself, love. You can't go bending and lifting in your condition,' she would say, and then call Maurice and tell him that I was stealing flowers from her garden.

I didn't tell Jessie about the letter. I thought it would upset her and she really didn't have to know that Dad was planning to marry. I replied to McDonald, McBride and Pringle that I had no idea where my real mother was and I was sorry I could be of no further assistance. Dad did get married but I didn't get an invitation to his wedding.

EIGHTEEN

My baby was due any day and I was getting nervous and excited. The previous months had dragged by and I was impatient to give birth – not least because I had put on three stones in weight and was suffering from excruciating back pain – and hold the child in my arms. My cases had been packed for more than four weeks and the layette had been washed and laid away in the new nursery. Quite unconsciously I had done what my father did for me, his firstborn: I bought a magnificent, navy-blue coach-built pram with white walled tyres and a huge, fringed sun canopy. My baby was going to have the very best from day one. Apart from the odd comment on my condition, Jessie took no interest in any of the preparations for the greatest event in my life so far.

As Jessie and I sat having a cup of tea in my kitchen the most appalling pain shot through me, causing me to cry out and double up.

'Jesus, it's starting, Jessie. Quick, call Derek!' I was panicking and afraid to move. All the instructions and advice I had been given over the last six months flew out of my mind.

Jessie was unruffled and sat watching me, a strange look coming over her face. 'Oh, it'll be hours yet. It won't just drop out.' She sounded snappy and busied herself clearing up the cups. The spasm passed.

'I'm scared, Jessie. Will you stay with me until Derek comes home?' My hand was trembling as I lit a cigarette. I hadn't felt the baby moving for a day or two, and in the back of my mind I was worried that the baby would be handicapped or, worse, dead. I was thirty-one and the hospital had written 'elderly prim' on my notes.

'Stop making such a bloody fuss. It's not the first and it won't be the last kiddie born.' I was in no mood to have a row with her, but I was taken by surprise by the bitterness in Jessie's voice. She had not spoken like that to me since I was about fourteen or to my sure knowledge to anybody else either. Jessie was what could be described as an appeaser, and if she did have strong opinions I never heard them. To the contrary, she could easily be bullied and I was constantly watching to see that she was not being taken advantage of. I looked at her and saw something in her eyes that I hadn't seen or noticed before.

'Jessie, sit down please!' She seemed not to have heard me and turned her back to me. As she stared out of the window I saw her shoulders heave up and down; she was crying. Awkwardly, I gently turned her to face me and was shocked to see the depth of pain and suffering in her tear-filled eyes.

'Tell me what's bothering you. Are you worried about the cancer coming back?'

I was trying to be as gentle as I could.

She shook her head. 'No, love, it's not the cancer ...' She couldn't go on.

I was really worried now. What on earth could be causing her so much anguish? 'Jessie, you have to tell me what's wrong. Whatever it is, it can be sorted out. Come on, nothing can be that bad, surely?' I handed her a tissue and waited while she dried her eyes. I listened with a sense of shock and pity as she told me her story.

'When your father came to lodge at my house I weren't looking for much out of life. He was so handsome and generous, and always smiling. When he told me that he loved me, I had a very hard decision to make. I had no life with Davie; he was a work-shy git, you know. I worked from morning till night, sometimes doing three jobs to make ends meet. Davie drank the money as soon as I earned it. Yes, it was a hand-to-mouth existence. I knew that if I stayed with Davie I would be dead before long – I had thought of topping myself, you know.'

I didn't interrupt, although I felt niggling pains in my stomach. I had to hear the rest and I was scared of breaking the spell. Jessie was walking through another time and another place where she had to go alone, and it was breaking her heart.

'You do remember my mam, don't you?' Jessie looked down at her bony hands. 'Well, I knew she were bad to you. I could have stopped her but I didn't. She were bad to me and all when I were a kiddie. But meeting your father gave me the strength to stand up to her and when I finally made the decision to leave Yorkshire with him I left my Myrna with her.' She paused for a few seconds whilst she dabbed her eyes. 'I told her that if she as much as harmed one hair on her head I would kill her, and I meant it!' She was looking at me now.

I couldn't say anything as the shock of her revelation registered. Jessie was a mother.

'Leaving Myrna, my precious little girl,' she put her hand across her mouth but a dry sob escaped, 'you know, after Myrna Loy, the film star – she was only nine, the same as you was – it broke my heart. I tried to get away to see her as often as I could. Remember when I went away for a few days? That's where I was. She has never forgiven me. I tried to like you, Evelyn, but, God forgive me, I just had to make you as miserable as I imagined Myrna was.'

I was stunned. I had not had the slightest idea that she was a mother. It had never occurred to me. Poor Jessie: all those years her heart had been crying for her daughter.

'I'm sorry,' was all I could say.

'I made the decision; no one else did. If I had pushed it, your father would have agreed to let me bring her. I'm glad in a way I didn't, though. Your father was hard on all you lot. That bloody case changed him; he was never the same. I'd have bleeding killed him if he had hurt my little girl.' There was a definite charge in my kitchen. The small room seemed to be filled with the accumulated misery she had suffered over the years.

'Why did you stay with him? It's not as though you were married to him,' I offered. After all, we had all got out the minute we could, and although I hadn't been happy at first with Derek, I was certain in my own mind that I would never have put up with a man as difficult as Dad.

'I made a promise to him; I never break a promise, you know me.'

It didn't seem a good enough reason to me. Jessie wanted to talk, so I let her continue. I owed her that much at least.

'When Des asked me to go to Ireland with him and look after his six children, he told me that his kids needed a mother. He told me that you lot had been committed to the State industrial schools when your mam had walked out on her family the day after Christmas. Apparently your granny and her other daughters had offered to care for you all. Your father had refused: as far as he was concerned they no longer existed. Your father was under the impression when he told me this that as he had voluntarily signed the committal papers he could take you home when he wished. He knew that time was running out. He explained that some of the schools were notorious for cruelty and abuse, in particular the Christian Brothers who ran Artane and the Sisters of Mercy at Goldenbridge in Dublin. You, being the oldest, would be transferred from the care of the Sisters of Charity and the Poor to one of the harsher regimes when you reached your tenth birthday, which wasn't far away. He needed someone to look after his kids so that he could bring you all home as soon as possible.'

Jessie stared for a few seconds into the bottom of her teacup. Briefly I wondered if she was trying to read the tea leaves, as she often claimed she could do. She looked squarely at me as she told me her story and for once I knew she was not exaggerating or embellishing the details, as was her habit when telling tales – 'romancing' Dad called it.

He had made it all sound so easy; he had even hinted that he was falling in love with her.

Jessie had been trapped in her miserable marriage for more than ten years. The war years, when David was called up, had brought some relief. She had worked in the munitions factory and for the first time in her life she had her own money. She even joined the girls from the factory when they went dancing. Jessie had enjoyed a couple of flirtations with visiting soldiers. 'Nothing serious, though – just enough to make me feel attractive and wanted. There was definitely no sex.' She gave a little shudder.

But when David was demobbed at the end of the war, he was more morose than ever and drank too much. He wouldn't get a job. He played up and exaggerated his war experience; Jessie found out later that he had been stationed in Scotland in the navy supplies store. She resigned herself to a life of toil and drudgery with this miserable man. Where could she go if she left him, she had often wondered.

By some miracle this big, handsome young Irishman had come into her life one Friday night when she had gone to the Horse and Hounds in the village square for her usual game of dominoes with some of the old regulars. She had been surprised when a handsome stranger told her that he was looking for her. She regretted having not washed her face or put on a little lipstick. She wished she had put something decent on to wear that night – she had just thrown one of David's old over-coats over her shoulders. The man was looking for 'digs' and at first Jessie refused him because he was Irish. Then she took a good look at him and decided that he wasn't the average thick-necked ruffian that most of the Irish building workers appeared to be and she offered him a room and board, cross-ing her fingers and hoping that she wouldn't live to regret her decision.

'When he asked me to go away with him I thought this would be my last chance for some happiness. But I did wonder how I would manage six kiddies and my own kiddie at my age; I am ten years older than your father, you know,' she added. Dad told her that I was a great little mother, and had been looking after my brothers since I had been practi-cally a babbie myself. He told her not to worry and promised that everything would be all right. She decided that she must take this chance, although the price was going to be high.

'My mother warned me that the "Irish git" would bring me nothing but heartache. I had to smile; this from a woman who had stood idly by when her new husband had beaten and abused me from the age of eleven, not offering a comfort-ing word or hug. This mother who had held my little finger-tips on the hot kitchen range to teach me a lesson about stealing a slice of meat when I was only six years of age, and who never allowed me to sit still and rest but had me skivvy-ing in the family chip shop without pay from the minute school was over until well past midnight. My mother's con-cern rang hollow.' Jessie was obviously still angry with her mother.

I understood. Her mother had demonstrated a cruel streak when she lived with us in Manchester. She would wait until I was present and with a great show of contempt for me, hand a sixpence to all the boys but not to me. Or she would make a wonderful stew and didn't mind telling me that I could make do with the two slices of bread and margarine that was our usual tea. Yes, I was well aware of how cruel her mother could be.

Jessie went on, 'I didn't care what Mam said. I was taking my chances with your father. She told me that she would see to Myrna. Happiness comes at a price, they say.'

When they left for Ireland, Jessie sat beside Dad as far back in the rear seat of the single-decker bus as she could. She imagined that everyone on the bus knew that she was running away; she struggled hard to bury the guilt and shame she felt as the bus noisily pulled itself up the steep hill out of the dark, deserted village square. As the little bus meandered across the bleak Pennine Moors towards Manchester, Jessie stared out into the darkness and allowed herself the luxury of a few tears.

'I weren't religious, but I asked God's forgiveness. Deep down I knew I was making a mistake, I suppose. When my reflection in the darkened window of the bus stared back at me, it was as though I was looking at someone else.'

Although Dad had made going to Dublin with him and looking after his children sound easy, within weeks of arriving in Dublin it was clear that he had been mistaken in believing that he could just collect us from the schools. The Minister of Education had written to him of me, 'In my view it would not be in the child's best interests to discharge her until suitable female assistance be procured.' Dad had exploded with rage, the first of many such rages Jessie was to witness over the years, and it sent shock and dread through her. A long drawn out legal battle ensued. Jessie was caught up in the middle of this – something she hadn't bargained for. Then there was Granddad, a cantankerous old man in Jessie's view, who wouldn't even allow her to clean the very dirty house she was expected to live in. When Dad went away for a week to work in the country, she hadn't been able speak to a single soul for the entire time as she didn't know anyone in Dublin. And on top of everything else she felt that I was hostile and belliger-ent towards her when she and Dad visited me, which of course I was. In all she decided that she had made a terrible mistake and maybe if she went back to England it wouldn't be too late. 'Your father caught up with me just as I was about to board the mail boat and begged me to stay. You know your father, he could cry at the drop of a hat, and I had promised him to help with you lot.'

She found me no easier when I came home and she built up a resentment towards me that triggered the dreadful row with Granddad about me. 'There you were, getting piano les-sons, and there was talk of sending you to the music school, to be an opera singer no less! Oh yes, your grandfather had grand ideas for you, and your father was agreeing with him. Well, it wasn't going to happen as far as I was concerned. My Myrna was without her mother and as I saw it if she couldn't have it you were not going to get it either.' She was getting fierce now at the memories. I didn't like to interrupt; there was nothing I could say or add. She told Dad that I caused trouble, that I was lazy and dirty, and that's why she was hard on me. She had even found it difficult to use my name. Dad said he would speak to his father but he didn't want to be bothered by this stupid carry-on and told Jessie to ease off me.

In the vicious row that went on for hours between Dad and Granddad – the row that I'd heard the tail end of – that dread-ful day my beloved Granddad went out of my life, Granddad told Dad that he was going to make sure that I got the musical education and that my days as a skivvy to him and Jessie were over. Jessie had tried to intervene but both men told her to mind her own 'bloody' business. To Jessie's relief, Granddad packed his bags and left. However, she didn't bargain on Dad blaming her for the whole fiasco, which did not improve their relationship.

'Most of the lads were OK but Dermot was just like you, and I saw myself being trapped as long as he was little. I was looking at another five years at least before I could get away with a clear conscience; well I was determined you were not going to get the better of me and that was for sure.'

I detected huge regret in her voice as her tone softened. Her guilt for numerous acts of cruelty was weighing heavily on her. I pitied her so much.

She had fully intended leaving when we had got to England. But she left it too late to go back to Yorkshire and had to put up with listening to Dad shouting and bawling for almost twenty years. There wasn't even any pretence of affection from him. She was sure that he was seeing other women; he never took her anywhere except to PayLess for the shopping, which he expected her to pay for. Dad told her that he was earning money when he went to the pub, but she never saw any of it. She put a ten bob note into her biscuit tin whenever she could spare it: the rainy-day money she prayed Dad wouldn't find.

After another contraction doubled me over I struggled to my feet and made a pot of tea. There was nothing I could say to Jessie at that moment. Although she had been responsible for some of the difficulties of her life, undeniably she had suffered at the hands of others and had borne her troubles with stoicism. I would see to it that she would enjoy the remainder of her life. We drank our tea in almost complete silence.

After an incredible thirty-seven-hour labour on the hottest day of the year my beautiful child entered the world. His minute fingers curled around my index finger and I promised him that nothing would ever harm him as long as I lived.

Five days later I stepped into my home carrying Ben. Jessie was waiting. She had filled the house with lovely flower arrangements to welcome me back.

I handed my precious baby to her. 'He needs a grandma.'

I didn't mind that her tears splashed on to his perfect little face.

AFTERWORD

When something upsetting happens, I am in the habit of saying to my son, 'But what will it matter in fifty years' time?' And my early life seems a long time ago now. When I am asked how I can remember details with such clarity, I say truthfully that one cannot forget trauma or great happiness.

In writing this memoir, I had to go to places I thought I had left behind long ago. Some of that journey was as painful as when I experienced the events the first time around. But the past shouldn't be allowed to colour the present and I have tried to live by that rule.

My father was unable to come to terms with the hand dealt to him by fate and tried to eliminate from his life anything or anyone that would hurt him.

If I have given the impression that he was a monster, forgive me; he was anything but. He was generous to a fault, kind-hearted, often very funny and his sense of humour was second to none. Despite his apparent cruelty to us, he was fiercely protective, and would have given his life for us, I am sure. None of this excuses his harsh treatment of us, but I have forgiven him completely. On his deathbed he told me that he had done nothing with his life. 'I'm sorry for all the trouble,' he said. He didn't say what trouble he meant, but we both knew he was talking about our miserable childhood in Manchester. No matter what he thought, he did a pretty good job of raising six children. We – my brothers and I – learned to be self-sufficient, honest and reliable and have all lived pretty fulfilled lives; and we have raised our own children with love and respect. He died when he was only sixty-two. Whatever the death certificate says, I think he just gave up the struggle for the happiness and the peace he was constantly seeking but never found. His six children kept an all-night vigil at his bedside as he painfully struggled towards that loneliest of journeys to death. I kissed him and said 'Goodbye, Daddy' and left him minutes before he died; I couldn't bear to see him lifeless, this big strong man who had by turns loved me and terrorised me and whom I never stopped loving. I know Our Lady is taking care of him in heaven.

Jessie outlived my father by almost ten years. She was a marvellous granny to my son and lavished love and protection on him. I used to tell her that she was spoiling him and she would shoot back proudly, 'Well, that's what grannies are for!' and totally ignore my complaint. The cancer continued to ravish her body and I lost count of the times I tried to prepare Ben for his granny leaving us. She would giggle like a schoolgirl each time the doctors reprieved her: 'They'll 'ave to shoot this old bugger.'

The truth is that the last twenty years of her life were her happiest. We developed an easy friendship, and when, just a few months short of her eightieth birthday, she was drifting off to her last big sleep, I held her skinny hand and told her that I loved her. 'Don't be afraid, love,' I whispered in her ear as she drifted off. I hope she heard me. I think she did, for a serene calm settled on her lined and worried face. Jessie had become my mother on the day I gave birth to my own child, and I think I really did love her.

As we cleared out her little house we laughed at finding Catholic pictures, Protestant Bibles and black witch paraphernalia. Jessie had taken no chances and booked a place into any heaven that would have her. The three-foot-high statue of St Jude, the patron saint of hopeless causes, is still with me. I didn't know what to do with it and found it impossible to throw it in the bin. He now sits in a corner of my study, keeping an eye on things for Jessie.

Often I have met men who tell me that they are not allowed to see their children after separating from their partners. I recently met a group of such men in Dublin. Their pain and suffering was such that it reached into my soul. I cried silently for these men and their children who are being forced to grieve unnecessarily and my prayers are with them. When Derek and I reached the painful conclusion that we were hurting each other as well as Ben by staying together, we included Ben in the discussions. Ben and I helped Derek to move into a tiny new bungalow just a few minutes' walk away, and although Ben was angry and frightened for a time, I overheard him telling his friends that he now had two houses he could live in. I remained close to Derek, even through his very brief and unhappy second marriage, and when he died suddenly at the ridiculously young age of fifty-eight I was devastated. Derek had developed diabetes and despite what his doctors told him he totally ignored his illness. Did he push the self-destruct button? My grief and guilt tore me apart until one night, about six months later, I had the most vivid dream. I was straightening Derek's tie and brushed down his coat lapels with my fingertips. 'Well, I must be off now. Don't worry; I'm fine,' he said as he lightly brushed my cheek with his lips and was gone. I awoke with tears streaming down my face, but my heart was at peace.

I have had no contact with my mother for more than thirty years and, frankly, I don't think of her. She has not tried to contact me or my brothers since that day when I walked away from her, although it would have been easy for her. Kevin called to see her every few years when he lived in the same area of Glasgow as she did. She told me one day when I first found her that she had told her doctor that the baby she was expecting, ten months after she had left my father was her first child. Did she convince herself that this was true?

As for me, I achieved what my father never found. I am supremely happy with Michael and am grateful to his very 'ordinary' family for allowing me into their tribe: his wonderful mother and father, John and Mary, his very funny brother Keith, a kind and dedicated teacher, and his gentle sister Moira. I am boringly proud of my talented musician son, Ben, who has been the sunshine in my rainy days. His sense of fun and youthful exuberance have seen me through some difficult times. Now he is a father himself and lives happily with his sweet and pretty partner Pamela.

I treasure and adore my little grandson Joshua and hope he has an easy path thorough this great journey we call life. But I intend to stick around until he is well on his way.

My darling grandson

Joshua, you captured my heart on that glorious day in March just four short years ago.

As I held you close I vowed to protect and love you for ever.

Your world will be so different from mine; at least that is my fervent hope.

You will not know poverty or the pain of being separated from all those you love and all that is familiar;

The despair of not knowing if there could ever be any happiness in this world should never be yours.

But don't feel sad for me because as I gaze back down the years I realise that all that happened, good and bad, made the rich tapestry that is you and I.

Grandma